The
LARRY NICHOLS
Story

Damage Control:
How to Get Caught with Your Pants Down and Still Get Elected President

Authorized Biography by
David M. Bresnahan

CAMDEN COURT PUBLISHERS, INC.
SALT LAKE CITY

CAMDEN COURT PUBLISHERS, INC.
7304 South 300 West, Suite 202
Midvale, UT 84047

The Larry Nichols Story—Damage Control
Copyright © 1997 David M. Bresnahan

Back cover photo by David M. Bresnahan

ISBN: 1-890828-10-6

First Edition: Spring 1998

PRINTED IN THE UNITED STATES OF AMERICA.
10 9 8 7 6 5 4 3 2 1

To
Kerry and Beth

To
Rhonda,
Michael, Katie, David, and Joseph

Contents

Introduction   *1*
1. Larry Nichols   *17*
2. Damage Control Really Works   *37*
3. Money Laundering   *65*
4. On Clinton and Sex   *85*
5. Clinton's Circle of Power   *109*
6. Many Investigations, No Results   *135*
7. Talk Radio   *161*
8. Nicholisms   *177*
9. Marching Orders   *195*
Appendix   *199*

Acknowledgments

Larry Nichols would like to acknowledge the following talk show hosts for the assistance they give him in getting his message to the American public. These are the ones who have given him the most time on the air over the years. Many hundreds of others have also had him on as a guest, but the ones on this list have gone above and beyond the call of duty by putting Larry on the air very frequently.

Keith Rush—One of the few hosts who has a special way of picking at me, but there is no one better than "the original Rush".

Bob Grant—Thanks to Bob, I was able to penetrate a whole new audience I had never spoken to before. Many more people heard my story because of him.

Pastor Ernie Sanders—Ernie is not afraid of anything as long as he's got the Lord on his side. He even came to Arkansas so he could tell his audience what it's really like.

Russ and Dee Fine—This couple truly has command of the Birmingham radio market. They have a unique relationship with their audience, and they introduced me to their audience, who really are their friends.

Jim and Rose Quinn—Jim's program is always early in the morning for me. Jim and Rose have an incredible show.

Mike Segal—Mike helped me to be heard in the northwest market, where he is king.

Geoff Metcalf—Geoff's San Francisco market is one you'd expect to be solidly liberal. Yet he has a huge conservative audience and it's a credit to him.

Ray Briem—What do you say about a legend? His show has such a large, concerned audience that he literally put me on the map and has stuck with me.

George Putnam—George has the most loyal following in the nation. People in his audience love him, and justifiably so. There's no one more honest in delivery in the country. By putting me on his program, he gave me a huge audience. But more than that, I am truly honored just to have him as a friend.

Mike Reagan—When I started trying to get into talk radio, I went station by station though every little and big town in the nation. It was only when Mike Reagan introduced me nationally that I actually gained credibility. He has that kind of national position and reputation. Mike has a quality program that gives him credibility, and when he interviewed me he passed some of that credibility on to me. I must also say that I credit Mike Reagan for saving my life (details in Chapter 7).

Zoh Hieronomus—Zoh has been able to take me right into Washington, D.C. Her program is the lone conservative voice penetrating right into Washington. There is not a more conservative voice in D.C. radio than Zoh, plus she's a good friend.

Warren Duffy—Duffy gave me an entry to the California Christian audience. He has an incredible following that brought me a whole new world of new friends.

Jazz McKay—It's not everyday that you see a long-haired motor-cycle biker doing a conservative talk show. This man is crazy, but he's absolutely incredible.

Marlin Maddux—Marlin is another host who has built a solid core of followers over many years. When he allowed me to be on his show, it meant more to me than just being able to get my information out. It meant that I had arrived. It meant that I was somebody, because truly he is an institution in talk radio and has been for years.

Vic Eliason and Jim Schneider—Vic has helped me, even though he was under incredible attack himself. He and Jim have a huge Christian and secular audience. When others have let you down, Vic and Jim will be right there with you.

Dr. Stan Montieth—Dr. Stan is a true gentleman, a true conserva-tive, and has a gracious style that makes him unique in the broadcast community.

Stan Solomon—Stan has an energy and drive that, when things were down, could pump me up and fire me up like nothing else could. He goes after the issues, tells the truth, and doesn't back down. He can stand with me anytime.

Steve and Chuck Williams—Steve and Chuck will always have a special place in my heart because Steve tried to get me into broadcasting on his own station. Chuck continually helps me keep the people in Pensacola informed. It is a truly Christian station all around.

Jack Cole—I remember Jack Cole the first time I did an interview with him. He was yelling at me because I would dare to come out against Bill Clinton and talk about the womanizing issue. He hit me hard, but fair. I proved myself to him and now he knows I am telling the truth. I am grateful to him.

Lou Epton—If there's ever been a definition of class, it's Lou Epton. If there's ever been a definition of warmth, it's Lou Epton. You can't be around him without feeling at ease and honored. He is truly a great talent in the world of broadcasting.

Steve Quayle—When times were bad and it didn't seem like anyone else was helping, Steve asked his audience to help me. I'll never forget that. He needed the help for himself, but he passed it on to me. There are not many people in the world today who will do that.

Jeff and Marsha Baker—Jeff and Marsha tried to give me a start by giving me my own program (something I didn't do well). I'll always be grateful to them for having the confidence in me to let me try.

Jack Christy—As long as I live I'll remember sitting on the curb at LAX when Jack was the only one who would give me a ride. We just sat and talked. That means a lot to me still today. He's always there to help.

Don Wiedeman—Don took the time, when he was building his station, to let me come on and be a part of his program. He single-handedly allowed me to develop an audience that I would have never reached otherwise, in an area that I would have never even thought about. Unfortunately, his station burned and I wish him Godspeed in getting back on the air.

Bo Gritz—What do you say about a true American hero? Bo tells it like it is and stands on the firm ground that he will defend America with his dying breath. I'm awfully grateful that he allowed me time to be on with him, just to be able to stand by a true American hero.

Jack McLamb—Much like Bo, Jack is an American hero. He is truly out to defend the country. He stands with and behind law enforcement all over the country, a leader in a world without leadership.

Tom Valentine—Tom has developed a reputation of being on the cutting edge of getting the truth out. I'm excited when I'm with him and he allows me the time to tell my story. He helped me gain credibility.

Bob Heckler—Many a night we would spend building a relationship with his audience, and me with Bob. I'll always be grateful to him. There is no better talk show host on this planet than Bob.

Peter Ford—Although I haven't done many programs with Peter, I can't leave him off this list. He would have me on anytime, but since I was on his station with Ray and George, there was no sense of overkill. Peter is a true patriot in the best standing of any in the world.

"Mason in the Morning"—"Mason in the Morning" is one of those shows that makes you feel good to be an American. I'm so grateful to be able to tell my story to his audience. He's a good friend.

Jane Chastaine—Jane is another one of the special people. She has a very loyal following. She is very careful whom she puts on and careful that all her guests tell the truth. She helped me by letting me tell and prove my story on her show.

Beverly LaHaye—Beverly activated a whole new society of people for me when she was gracious enough to allow me to be on her program. She is one of the strongest voices in America.

Rush Limbaugh—Even though I haven't been a guest on his program, he has been a huge force in opening up the world of conservative talk radio. All talk show hosts owe a lot to Rush Limbaugh. He is the father of modern conservative talk radio, and without him there would not be as many other talk show hosts out there today. He created the means for us to tell our story.

Chuck Harder—I did his program early on when I first began trying to tell America my story. Chuck helped me in those early days.

David Bresnahan—Dave and I entered this book project on our word. We haven't even had a handshake because we've done it long-distance, just on our word. People tell you a man's word isn't worth anything anymore. Yes, it is. I'm proud to have Dave as a friend. I'm proud to have him working on this project with me. It should show a sign of how much I believe in him that I'll take his word for the contractual arrangements for this project.

Introduction

A Modern Paul Revere

Over 200 years ago, a courageous American went on a midnight ride to warn citizens that the British were coming. He knew the danger that awaited and knew that if his fellow citizens were aware of that danger they would stand in defense of their freedom. Like Paul Revere, Larry Nichols is on a midnight ride as he shouts his warning of danger not from the back of a horse, but from the radio air waves.

Larry's been beaten to a pulp more than once. He's been threatened. Attempts have been made to buy him off. His lawyer nearly died from a beating he received. Employers won't hire him because of threats and intimidation. Local business people and others have been told to have nothing to do with him, or suffer the consequences.

With no job and no employer who will hire him anywhere in Arkansas, Larry lost his cars, home, and all material possessions. Despite years of persecution and constant harassment, he won't give up his quest. Even the offer of money as his house was being foreclosed did not persuade him to quit. He says he knows that one day he will succeed because he won't give in. To preserve a future in a land of freedom for his family, he says he will not let his enemies stop him.

Larry Nichols, 47, of Conway, Arkansas, is perhaps the only person in America who has a chance of dethroning President Bill Clinton. The evidence and witnesses he has compiled are overwhelming. Larry claims the crimes and corruption of Clinton can be proven by the documents he has collected, which fill 40 boxes and are stored in more than one secret location. Indeed, a sampling of the documents he has made public appear to verify his claims.

Larry was a Clinton loyalist for many years. During Clinton's early terms in state office, he helped run damage control to keep Clinton out of trouble, thereby keeping him in office. Larry helped him willingly, and he did it well. The relationship between them lasted until the day he confronted Clinton about evidence he had discovered, revealing that drug money may have been laundered through a state-operated financial agency.

Larry is the first to admit he himself was no saint. He was willing to use the damage control tactics described in this book to further the political career of Clinton, with the hope it would be rewarding financially for him to do so. He considered his damage control work for Clinton to be "just politics," until he discovered evidence which convinced him that money laundering and other crimes were involved. The day he confronted Clinton with his suspicions was the day Larry's life turned upside down.

Congressional and senate investigative committees have copies of the evidence provided by Larry. Special Prosecutor

Kenneth Starr has the evidence. Larry has a list of secret witnesses willing to come forward but only by public subpoena and only under oath. They fear that they may be in danger if they come forward any other way. Most of them have been ignored by the investigators. Not only is Larry courageous in his efforts to expose his evidence, but he is an extremely talented detective, able to find information and witnesses no one else has been successful in locating. Larry makes himself available to the public and the press by freely giving his home phone and address to everyone. As a result, he spends 10, 12, even 20 hours a day being interviewed on radio talk shows from one end of the country to the other. After six years pursuing that effort to inform the public, Larry has a growing number of supporters. Time and time again the claims he has made have been proven true as the mainstream press reluctantly prints the results of investigations. That's not to say he hasn't also accumulated his critics. They are not large in number but they are very vocal, usually ranting and raving from an emotional viewpoint rather than addressing the factual evidence presented.

Indeed, it would appear that his greatest protection is his constant and continuous appearance on talk radio. As he has become increasingly more well known, the beatings by enemies have lessened, while the general harassment has increased. His opposition appears to have altered its tactics. Public attention has grown so strong that if someone harmed Larry, the talk shows would instantly blame people loyal to Clinton. To avoid that blame, Larry believes Clinton loyalists may be keeping an eye on him "just in case some nut tries something crazy".

First Contact
My first contact with Larry Nichols was in early 1995 as the host of a local talk show in Salt Lake City. Our station was an affiliate of the nationally syndicated Michael Reagan Talk

Show, the number one evening talk show in the nation. More than once I had heard Reagan interview Larry and was fascinated by the information he gave. Because I was a member of the Utah House of Representatives, my listeners made a special effort to keep me well-informed on a number of issues with the hope and expectation that I could accomplish a little more than the average talk show host.

One day such a listener greeted me outside the studio as I got off the air. He handed me a video tape and said, "You have to promise me you'll watch this before you put your head on your pillow tonight. I can't let you take this unless I have your word that you'll watch it tonight." I looked at the tape and saw that it was "The Clinton Chronicles", the very tape I had heard mentioned on the Reagan show when Larry had been a guest. My journalistic curiosity was high so I made the promise. The man did not identify himself but instead just said, "I'll be listening to your show to hear your reaction." He never returned for his tape and to this day I have no idea who he was.

Where's the Honor and Respect?

The tape was a shocker, deeply upsetting. As a reporter and an elected official, I had learned a great deal about corruption in government over the years, but this tape hit hard because it was talking about the most honored position in the world. The president of the United States of America was being accused of very major crimes. Regardless of political affiliation, I was taught from my youth to honor the office of president and treat that person with respect.

Indeed, I had an opportunity to meet briefly with President Clinton in the summer of 1994 at the White House, during the time I was a Republican candidate for the Utah House. Despite our opposite political affiliation, I considered it an honor and privilege to meet the president and first lady. The meeting was a cordial one and, although I used the meeting to criticize the president's health care plan, I criticized the plan, not him.

If the video tape I had watched was even half true, it shook the very foundation of my trust and faith in the highest office in the land. The implications were enormous, not only of corruption by Clinton, but also by those who were helping to cover it up.

As a college student, I had my faith in that office diminished when the nation went through the Watergate hearings. At that time, my father, a longtime Democrat and union member, discovered a derogatory poster of President Nixon on my wall (an unflattering photo captioned, "Would you buy a used car from this man?"). "Regardless of what he may or may not have done, he's our president and deserves our respect. If we don't agree with him, if we don't like the things he's done, we'll have our chance to elect someone else soon enough," my father chided me. I took the poster down and remembered the lesson.

The first time I ever voted in an election was in 1972. I ended up voting for Nixon after personally interviewing George McGovern twice when he visited Lowell, Massachusetts, where I was the news director of a local radio station. Nixon won in every state that year except Massachusetts.

I remember vividly the day Nixon resigned. I watched him give his parting speech before getting on the helicopter, and because I was alone, I did not stop the tears of disappointment that came as I watched. They were not tears for Nixon the man but tears of sadness that the office I had been taught to revere had been tarnished so badly.

In the years that followed, presidents came and went and my trust and faith were somewhat rebuilt (in spite of my political differences with each). Now suddenly in 1995, I found myself confronting what seemed to be very strong, documentable evidence that President Clinton had a history of corruption which would bring discredit to that office far beyond the comparatively minor offenses of Richard Nixon. As I watched the video a second time, I invited my wife, Rhonda, to view it with me. She has always helped me to see through hype and exaggeration, and I knew her evaluation would keep me from overreacting. Her reaction was stronger than mine. She just shook her head and repeated, "How sad. How sad."

As a reporter I had learned to check my sources. By transferring my journalism skills to talk radio, I had earned the respect of my audience because they knew when I reported something to them I had first checked it out myself. I got on the phone to Mike Reagan, whom I had come to respect as a talk show host with a similar desire to get to the facts. He assured me that Larry was for real and the evidence valid. I was given Larry's number to set up an interview.

It was then that I learned something that continues to astonish me to this very day: Larry was broke and not making a dime from the marketing of any video tape or book. Mike assured me that Larry was not paid for his appearance on "The Clinton Chronicles" and wasn't even getting a percentage from the sales. I called the producers of the video, who confirmed that fact.

Talk show hosts are inundated each day with requests from book authors for interviews so they can promote their work. Most guests on talk radio, speakers at conservative political events, and promoters of one worthy cause or another have something to sell. They often exaggerate the facts to create fear and a sense of urgency, thereby motivating their audience to buy their books, tapes, manuals, and newsletters. It has become a profitable industry, and many who began with a sincere desire to promote a worthy cause or issue find themselves caught up in the profits of marketing to conservatives hungry for such materials. Much is being sold in the interest of profit without attention to verifiable fact.

My skepticism was put to rest when I had the chance to

speak with Larry by phone and listen as he responded to the questions of some of my skeptical listeners while a guest on my show. I let them have at him and Larry held his ground well. He defended his claims against the Clintons as well as his contention that he was not making any money from the sale of the tape. In fact, unlike most other guests with something to sell, he never asked me to give out a toll-free order line or any form of instructions on how to get a tape. His interview, much to my amazement, was truly intended to inform, not promote a product. He was a news source, not a promoter of conspiracy books and tapes. The phones never stopped ringing and every line was full throughout the two-hour show. At the end of the show, I told listeners to tune in to Mike Reagan's show, which followed mine each day. There, Larry is a regular guest, often interviewing more than once a week.

Mike will tell you that Larry is a regular because he is a constant source of factual information about a continually developing story of corruption and abuse. In fact, Larry was heard so often on Reagan's show, and therefore on my station, that I chose not to have him back too often for fear of listeners would hear him too much, thus creating an overkill situation. Instead, listeners could call me and react to what they had heard on Reagan.

In 1996 my show became nationally syndicated and, in the early part of 1997, I interviewed Larry several more times for my national audience. Those interviews led to side discussions by phone and an interview for an article in my monthly newsletter. As I became more aware of Larry's incredible dedication in the face of enormous, unrelenting persecution, I felt impressed to help him further his efforts to inform the American people of the corruption taking place.

Tell the Truth

When I called Larry in April 1997 and offered to write a book about him, he agreed after careful consideration. He gave me complete freedom to write anything I wanted with only one requirement: it had to be the absolute truth—no hype or exaggeration. He very firmly demanded that I agree, saying, "If you find out on any point that I have exaggerated or that I have deceived you, intentionally or unintentionally, I demand that you put in the book that you caught me."

Larry made me agree that if I ever discovered something was not true, that I would tell the world of his failure to be honest. He promised me that he would not make any claim in our interviews that he could not support with documentation and that he would present his evidence upon request.

With that agreement in place, I began interviewing him by phone late each evening. It was a challenge only because of his high demand. Hardly a day would go by when I wouldn't speak with him at least for a few minutes. Often he would have to tell me that he was fully booked with talk shows. As I got to know him in this way, his dedication and effort became much more real to me as I witnessed him in action actually going from one talk show to the next from dawn to dusk. How he is able to sustain such an effort day after day is beyond my understanding. As a talk show host, I know how draining it can be to maintain a two- or three-hour show day after day. Larry is a guest on talk shows hour after hour, day after day, all with only one goal: expose the crimes he claims Clinton has committed with the hope that justice will be served.

And so I had to be patient. Each day I would call for a brief chat and in the evening I would call at the appointed hour, hopeful that some talk show host had not beaten me to him. Sometimes when I was lucky enough to get him to myself, I would detect how tired he was and couldn't bring myself to impose on him. I would tell him to go to bed and leave the interview to another night.

The next day I would discover that after I had hung up the night before, he had received another call to be on a talk show and stayed up even later. Often he would just keep going until he would literally fall asleep at the phone.

Once, while discussing the details of an aspect of Kenneth Starr's investigation, I interrupted Larry to ask a question. When I finished and awaited his response, all I got was the sound of his breathing. Over and over I called to him, with no response. Knowing that he has been beaten up and threatened time and again, I feared the worst when the phone was suddenly hung up!

My return calls to him on both of his lines went unanswered. Finally, after ten frightening minutes, Larry answered the phone with a very groggy "Hello?" He had fallen asleep Right in the middle of talking to me! It was both a relief and a concern at the same time. The man was absolutely exhausted, but would he hang up and go to bed? No. He apologized profusely and insisted that we continue until he finished what he wanted to tell me. To my amazement, he resumed our discussion right where we left off without being reminded of what he had last said or what my question was.

What began as a newsletter article, now expanded into over 100 hours of taped interviews. The more I learned, the more I asked. Just transcribing each interview took all the time I could spare. Meanwhile, my own daily talk show had stopped in June to free up my time and enable me to keep my business going so as to pay the bills. Even then there was so much information that there seemed to be no end in sight to the questions I had for Larry. Besides, the story I was writing about wasn't even close to being over and was developing nearly every day.

Finally, in September, I realized an investigative report with all the details of scandal after scandal would have to wait. There were plenty of books giving many of the details, but this book had to do something no other had done. The American people needed to know something more than the details of corruption. They needed to know how Clinton was so successful at deceiving so many. Knowing what his tactics are would go a long way toward helping people to not be deceived any longer.

My interviews with Larry opened my eyes to the fact that Clinton is a master politician. The methods he uses aren't so very special, it's just that he has perfected them beyond what anyone has done in the past. Understanding these methods enabled me to see right through them, and I decided that if I were to make any contribution, this would have to be it. Not a tell-all book, but rather a detailed description of political corruption and how it is packaged and sold to the public as something good and beneficial. One of Clinton's own staff called him "an incredibly good liar," and I needed to write a book on how he lies and gets away with it.

Time to Meet

With that realization, I excitedly called Larry and told him that I would need only one more interview—in person. Finally we would meet face to face, not in Arkansas but in California, where a group had invited him to come and speak.

Larry and Arkansas State Trooper Larry Patterson had six speaking engagements sandwiched between press interviews over a period of just four days. Even though I was there the entire time, getting a moment alone with either of them was next to impossible. Finally my chance to spend some quality time with Larry came on the last day. From the time of the last presentation until his flight home, there was a block of five hours. He was absolutely exhausted and painfully ill, but despite how tired and physically uncomfortable he was, Larry gave me his time, as did Trooper Patterson.

Being with him in person further verified all my previous impressions. His sincerity and dedication were obvious. He was genuine, without hype or exaggeration of any sort. In fact, I learned of numerous people with whom he has stopped associating due to their tendency to stray from the facts. He is determined to never give information that isn't fully verifiable. Time and time again I, along with others, have tried to compliment Larry only to be told by him that he is not the hero people make him out to be. He is the same person in an interview on the air as he is in private. Journalists know that the more time they spend interviewing a subject, the more that person lets his hair down and exposes his true character. Larry has been consistent throughout.

Larry Patterson is of similar character. He recognized his previous errors while he served on Governor's Security in the Arkansas State Police for more than six years, during which he says he felt pressured to give in to Clinton's demands to bring him women in order to preserve his job. Although criticized by the press for his delay in coming forward about Clinton's alleged womanizing, Patterson has demonstrated a sincere desire to correct his earlier failure to come forward and has paid a price in his career for speaking out. The story he tells in subsequent chapters is by itself an astonishing tale of rampant immoral conduct by Clinton. Combined with the details of corruption given by Nichols, it is a devastating tale of a president both men have labeled as sinister and evil. Indeed, it is a tale, if true, of the most sophisticated white-collar crime in American history.

Larry knows what evidence the congressional committees and Starr have because they got most of it from him. Much of that evidence has not been made public for fear that bringing it out now will jeopardize the investigations. Hence, Larry is holding off revealing parts of what he has compiled. He has taken the proper precautions to make sure that if something happens to him, the evidence remains preserved. Those precautions include not telling me about secret witnesses and evidence to avoid the chance I would compromise those items. Instead, he has promised a complete tell-all book with all the details and copies of the evidence if the current investigations come to naught. If that happens, and it looks more and more like it will, Larry wants the American people to know what evidence these committees have so the people can judge for themselves the extent of the corruption in Washington.

Larry believes that the corruption will continue if its methods continue to work so well. It will fail if its methods just don't work anymore. He is a light shining on those who prefer to operate in darkness. Larry knows that Clinton, and those who operate like him, will fail when their methods of deception are exposed to the people of this great country.

We can all relate to a salesman trying to twist our arms using old-style sales tactics. Salespeople all go to seminars to learn to sell and eventually they all tend to use the same methods. It doesn't take long for the public to start to recognize the same trite sayings being used by one sales person after another. The result is we are less likely to buy based on some persuasive tactic, but rather we make our choice based on the facts of the matter, at least until the sales people go to a new seminar and learn a new way to twist arms.

Expose How They Do It

Stopping corrupt politicians is as simple as recognizing their tactics. True, exposing them in detail in a book can provide a manual for Clinton wannabes, but once the public knows their tricks, Clinton and those who copy him will all fail miserably. Once the public is aware of the methods, when we can see politicians in action, point to them, and say, "Look, they're using that rope-a-dope tactic we read about," then and only then will their efforts to deceive fail, because we will all see right through them. The people will no longer be fooled.

Not only has Larry given us an inside look at the tactics of the damage control team of Bill Clinton, he has provided a sure fire method to counter attack. He knows how to deflate the damage control team and empower the people to demand truth and accountability from their elected representatives. What he presents is not a debate over political ideologies. His accusations run to both sides of the political aisle. He is not spouting off conservative Republican rhetoric and joining the throngs of Clinton bashers who bash only for purposes of partisan positioning. Larry stands apart from the crowd because he calls a spade a spade, as you will soon see in the pages ahead. In fact, he is perhaps one of the Republican leadership's biggest critics. While accusing Clinton of a whole string of high crimes, he points another finger at the Republicans he claims are covering it all up.

Damage control is a common practice by politicians of all types at all levels. Larry teaches us what they do, how they do it, and why it works so well. He identifies Clinton as the most effective at these tactics, but clearly illustrates that Clinton has many, many alliances that cross party lines who use these same damage control tactics. The sad realization also comes to light that Clinton has many willing students among politicians who aspire to gain his skills of deception rather than learn to be responsible leaders.

Disclaimer

This book is the authorized biography of Larry Nichols. It is not an attempt to rehash the endless details coming out about the scandals in the White House. Anyone seeking such information and detail can find what they need in other books and a growing number of news articles.

The reader will notice that throughout this book many names have been left out. Larry has made the names known to me and has supplied me with any evidence I have requested, except for in instances for security reasons. Opposition to what Larry is doing is so intense that I have agreed with his request to withhold names when not doing so could lead to harassing lawsuits and other tactics to stop him from continuing his pursuit of the truth and exposing it to the American public. His enemies are looking for the smallest excuse to attack him, and I don't wish to supply them with ammunition.

The tapes and notes compiled for this book have been turned over to Larry for his use as he wishes. I do not want to be in possession of materials that could be used by his enemies to discover sensitive details discussed in the preparation of this book. Everything in this book comes from interviews and I have done my best to attribute each source.

Obviously, I am biased, as I happen to think the world of Larry Nichols and regard him as an American hero. I would like to share everything I have learned from him in this book so each reader can know him in the same way I do, but to do so would be impractical. Larry and I will certainly be criticized by Clinton loyalists, by his enemies, and my political enemies. We must protect witnesses who are yet to come forward, to protect evidence that has not yet been made public, and to protect Larry. I have witnessed enough to believe that there are those who would leap at the chance to file suit against him for any excuse they can find in an effort to divert his time and resources. They will scrutinize every word in this book over and over until they find some way to attack. I have made every effort to minimize their ability to do so.

For those who are fans of Larry, I'm sure you will understand the decision to not disclose names at this time. For readers who are just becoming aware of Larry and his work, please reserve judgment until you have read this book in its entirety so that you may evaluate what he is doing from a more complete understanding of what he is up against. The remaining investigations in congress and by Kenneth Starr are not yet completed, and every attempt has been made to not compromise those efforts. No evidence or legal strategy has been revealed here that has not been discussed by others in the public forum.

Nothing in this book is to be construed as an accusation of any crime or wrongdoing by anyone. Only a court of law can decide if anyone did anything wrong. Any claims made in this book should be taken with the understanding that the claims are made on the basis that if the evidence thus far available is correct, it may be concluded that a possible crime has been committed. No intentional effort has been made to damage the character of any individual. Nothing has been stated in this book that hasn't already been said in other media.

1
Larry Nichols

Many people have mysteriously died who knew about various aspects of the alleged corruption surrounding Bill and Hillary Clinton. There are those who believe that these people died because someone wanted to prevent them from telling their story. Secret witnesses, who have not yet testified, are in constant fear for their lives. Larry has been beaten savagely more than once, arrested on trumped up charges, and been threatened repeatedly. He believes the only way witnesses to Clinton corruption can live is to come forward and tell their story, on the record under oath. He has convinced many to do so but many more still need to.

Later you will read the incredible tale of one such witness who had to be placed in hiding by Kenneth Starr's special investigation. Why? According to Larry, it was to protect the witness from being killed by those who are loyal to Clinton and want to eliminate that witness. It is frightening to imagine that a U.S. special investigator had to protect a witness from being killed by people loyal to the president of the United States.

Larry hasn't been killed yet, but he has suffered immensely because of the efforts he has made to undermine Bill and Hillary Clinton. To understand his motivations and the sacrifice he is willing to make, we must first begin by getting to know him. We need to get under his skin and find out what makes him tick, how he thinks. He is truly unique and his story is fascinating, whether you love or hate Bill Clinton, be you Democrat or Republican.

The Price of Being a Hero

Larry has indeed been willing to sacrifice everything he had in this world. He says it's the reason he is winning his battle to expose the alleged crimes of the Clintons and have them brought to justice. Beatings, intimidation, harassment, and offers of cash have not influenced him to change his course of action. The loss of his job, no prospect of a new job, and the subsequent loss of his home and possessions have not swayed him. His wife, Kerry, and daughter, Beth, have bravely and patiently had to endure all of this with him, and they must be given tremendous credit for their support to Larry.

"Because I have sacrificed everything, they can't get to me. I have nothing left," Larry explained to me. At first I thought he was exaggerating, but then I found out Larry Nichols never lies, misleads or exaggerates (unless he's "rolling in the mud", something we'll learn about that later in this chapter.) There is nothing that will make Larry give up or get him to leave Clinton alone. There has never been a more motivated, dedicated, driven man on earth than him. Does he believe he can save the nation? Change the world? Cleanse the earth of evil? No. He is surprisingly realistic.

"All I want to do is expose the crimes of Bill and Hillary to the people of this nation. I want them brought to justice, even though that's not likely—the system is so corrupt. All I can do is expose the evidence, but the courts are out of my hands. I won't stop until that happens. The people need to know what's going on. If this country is to be saved, it will be up to the people to save it, not me," he said matter-of-factly.

The Nichols family is now living in a small, rented home in Conway, Arkansas, the town where Larry was raised as a boy and has lived most of his adult life. Life is tough in his hometown; no one will hire him anywhere in the state—not because he's unqualified but because employers are scared. As he tells it, Arkansas has always operated under a good-old-boy network, and people have learned what happens if you don't do as you're told. They've been told not to hire Larry Nichols.

"Do you know what it would mean to me, to my family to make just a couple thousand a month?" Larry asked one night while discussing life in general after our interview for the night had ended. As our conversation progressed, I realized the personal insight I was getting about the "real" Larry Nichols was something that needed to be included here.

He told me, "A huge percentage of my problems at home would go away if I could show my wife and daughter that I'm contributing to their welfare. I know that I'm contributing to my daughter because I'm fighting so she can have a chance at a life like we've had. But she doesn't understand that. All my daughter and wife know is that they've had to do without. I have cost them everything. They are tired of paying. My wife told me tonight that she's not real proud of me because we're coming up on a bunch of bills and don't have the money to pay them. Our phone is about to be shut off and I don't have the money to pay it. It's a bad time around here."

Larry told me of the humiliation he felt just prior to our phone interview when he went to the store to get bread and

milk that night. There was virtually no money in the house so
he went to a nearby store with only change. Beth was too
embarrassed to go so Larry went. "Do you realize how
humiliating that is? I tried to get in a line with a young kid
because they don't realize what I have to do," he explained as
I began to feel really uncomfortable. My mind was searching,
my heart aching. How could I help take away some of the pain
he was feeling?

"The instant I get in line here comes someone I know, right
as I am having to count out change to pay for milk and bread.
That doesn't make you feel very good. Put that in your book;
talk about how it feels to be a hero. Then you'll start to feel
one percent of the pain I generate for my family every day.

"I drive a car that is my mother's. Kerry has a new car her
mother bought her because I couldn't. We could just not
afford to get a car for my daughter, Beth. My mother, bless her
heart, buys her a brand new truck because she worries about
her and all she has had to do without. Unbeknownst to me, my
mother got her a brand new truck. It is so nice. Instead of us
just jumping up and down and being happy, we're miserable
because we can't pay the gas for her to drive it. We can't even
pay the insurance—Mother pays that. She won't even come
over here because she starts crying. Thank goodness my
daughter is a daughter. She's 16. If she were a boy, she would
be afoot. Even my mother couldn't pay the insurance for
that," he said, trying to add some humor to a tense moment.

You Can't Dance with the Devil

Larry has been the most frequently heard guest on talk
radio since about 1991. He appears on literally hundreds of
shows, both local and national. Some have him on repeatedly
to update listeners as investigations progress. There are many,
many Larry Nichols fans all over the country. To them, Larry
is their hero, their knight in shining armor. But he says, "No,
I'm no leader. I can get the evidence, I can get the witnesses.

But the cavalry's not coming unless the people demand change. No one person can do it for them."

Many would fold under the kind of pressure he has faced and continues to deal with each and every day. He's even been enough offered money to save his home. Though I didn't need to ask why he didn't take it, I wanted to hear his response.

"You can't dance with the devil," he remarked in astonishment at my question. "If I do that, Clinton is going to succeed. We'd save our home, but Beth will have nothing. I knew that they would just destroy this nation in a second. I knew it. I knew it."

History

So where did Larry come from? What kind of background sent this modern Paul Revere on a midnight ride to warn our nation that corruption will destroy us?

He was born 29 July, 1950 and grew up right where he lives now, in Conway, Arkansas. His parents, Charles Derwood and Nelda Jo Nichols, had two boys and a girl. They taught their children some good old-fashioned values: hard work, honesty, respect, honor, morality, and right from wrong. Charles worked hard all his life to provide for his family and give his kids a better world than he grew up in. Larry reports his family members were not regular churchgoers, but they had strong fundamental beliefs in Christian principles, stemming from their membership in the Southern Baptist Church.

When the time came, Larry left for college. There, his studies were not top priority, so he and school parted company after a year. Next it was off to the Air National Guard, where it didn't take long for young Larry to get kicked out and into the Army Special Forces. He didn't like the military, but it was there that he matured and learned how to face the challenges of his life.

Larry had some excellent entrepreneurial skills at a young age. When he came out of the military, he returned home to

Arkansas, discovered a need, and filled it. At that time, if a business wanted a jingle to use in radio ads, the only place to have one made was New York or California, with a price tag of almost $50,000. He had a love of music along with some experience and knew he could offer a unique service at a great price.

Larry built his own small recording studio and began to create custom music for banks, charging only $2,000–$2,500 per jingle. He was a one-man show, doing everything from marketing to writing and performing the music. He quickly realized that after doing a jingle for one First National Bank, he could sell the same jingle to another First National Bank located in a different radio market. The banking laws were different then and most banks were small and independently owned. Before long, he had accounts with 200–300 banks.

Not only did he provide jingles, Larry learned what made radio advertising work and provided consulting as part of his fee. He knew the only way he would keep all those banks coming back for more would be to make sure they got response from their advertising. The studio was located in Little Rock and was called On Air Productions.

Larry learned that if he helped his clients succeed he would succeed. His formula was simple: "I started counseling with people that got the jingle. More than just giving them the music, I would help them design a schedule to get the frequency they had to have. Bottom line, make it work. In those days you see, that was kind of a novel idea. I learned early on that the ad agencies were nothing but rip-offs." Even at a young age he could spot when people were being treated unfairly.

He explained, "Let's say there was a time when you should not advertise. Well, an advertising agency wasn't going to tell you that because they had to make money off the media buy. So, I delved into all of that and, believe it or not, I got fairly accomplished, or certainly people thought so. People would call me up and I would design entire ad campaigns just to get somebody's jingle business."

Back in the late '70s, On Air Productions was the only recording studio in Little Rock. As the political season rolled around, the candidates all started to show up on his doorstep looking for help. As a young man, Larry had found fairly quick success and developed a good reputation. Now he not only had a successful business, but he found himself associating with politicians, which meant power. He enjoyed the attention and the life that went with it. It was exciting.

"I was a social climber. Morality didn't mean a heck of a lot back then," he confessed. "There were a lot of parties. It was a matter of doing what you had to do to get ahead. So I met the Clintons and all the others. There were quite a few people here that really made big money in the political business, and I got in among them. I met the movers and shakers. I did a lot of stuff for people and learned a lot of stuff. I learned that you can be the best person on earth, could have the best concepts, be the most moral, be the best thing for this nation, but there's a kicker: if you can't get elected, it doesn't mean a thing.

"So politicians would come in with their great little ideas, and I'd say, 'Look, be what you're going to be, but you're not going to get elected.' You know me now, and I was pretty much then as I am now. I've always been pretty much known for telling it like it is. Believe it or not, people like that. They respected that."

Clinton and Nichols

It was then that Clinton and Larry forged a relationship. Clinton would go to Larry's studio to design and produce his ads and create his strategy. It was in those sessions that he came to know Larry's natural talents, not only for creative advertising, but for overall strategy. and damage control tactics. These were skills that Clinton would value in the years ahead. He also learned that Larry was an extremely valuable asset in another important way: his business clients included nearly every bank in Arkansas, and bankers could be a big help to Clinton's political aspirations.

"I got to know him pretty well," Larry explained. "Clinton loved to go party. Everything was fun and games. And then I would help introduce him to the major people in different counties. I had the advertising budgets of most of the banks in Arkansas, plus the savings and loans. Obviously I could wield a pretty big stick when it came time to ask people for donations."

Community Turns Its Back

While we were talking on the phone, Beth, Larry's daughter, was in the other room with some of her friends, who were trying to convince her to return to school. Larry explained that he believed she was humiliated by kids, parents, and teachers in school because of him. Our discussion continued to reveal some of his inner workings.

"She made the pom-pom. It's like cheerleaders," he explained. "And, of course, come hell or high water, when the pom-poms were going to do their cheer, I was going to be there. When I was a kid and played football, my parents came and watched and it meant so much to me to have them up there. So I came and it really sucked, because up there in the stands I'd be, and everybody would be at the other end of the stands. It was pretty ugly. My daughter quit, saying it was because she didn't like it. But I know in my heart that she quit because she was embarrassed that I would come."

Crimes That Need Exposing

Larry's motivation to keep going is to win his reputation back with the people of his community, his mother, his father, Kerry, and Beth. To do that, he believes he must expose what he calls "the many crimes of Bill and Hillary Clinton". Larry wants to accomplish that goal in such a way that he will be vindicated by the same press that so savagely attacked him when he first voiced his claims. Ultimately, Larry would like to see the Clintons brought to justice, but admits that the system is so corrupt that it is unlikely to happen any time soon. Will this book help?

"I hope the book will help," Larry says. "They'll read it once. There's a society of people out there, like I told you before. If we just repeated something every other line, they would say the book is great. They don't even read it; they skim through and say it's great because they want to believe in me. But they want to believe in me so they can mentally deal with the situation at hand, which is, people cannot believe we're up a creek without a paddle. They always want to believe there's somebody out there to save them. The problem is that they really believe they can sit back and wait for a hero to save them so they don't have to do anything themselves, just like in the movies.

"You can tell the slant of our intellectual training because you see movies like *Star Wars*. It's a gigantic success, but why? Because it is an elementary tale of good versus evil, and the good guys win. Then up comes the newest thing: *Independence Day*. I mean, to think there's a super society up against a cropduster guy. If you can believe it, all of these ex-Vietnam pilots jump into jets and take on the bad guys. In the end, what happens? We win."

Larry sees the decay of moral values in society, the increasing level of immorality we as a society will tolerate from elected officials, and the disintegration of the traditional family structure as evidence that we are losing the battle of good versus evil. He wants people to realize that the cavalry's not coming, and if we sit back and wait for what's not coming, we'll lose it all. No one person can save this mess, and unless we, the people, take action, it will all be gone. The cavalry won't come unless we join the cavalry and ride in ourselves.

To Win, Get Down On Their Level

"Every day we seem to give something up in the interest of compromising our values. What has happened is we have gotten to a point where it used to be that if a politician were found to be corrupt, he was sent home in chains. Well, now we have gotten to a point to where we accept that all politicians are corrupt. We say that and mean that, yet the fact that we can say it and not do anything about it is exactly why we are losing. And all the fairy tales and rationalizations that you want to make are not solving the problem. Our politicians have now become corrupt because we have made it acceptable. There are some in there who are not, who are hanging on, but they are far, far, far in the minority. And the system of governing has been so perfected that even a good guy has to run several gauntlets. It's very tough to run the gauntlets and come out. So what happens? Even good people say, 'Look, in the interest of accomplishing overall good, I may have to go along with something that I'm not all that strong on, but if I lose this battle over this little thing then I'm out of here and then the overall good is over.'"

The sad truth is, Larry's right. We won't stop Clinton unless we are willing to get in the mud with him. The good, Christian, moral, conservative Americans who have spoken out against Clinton the loudest won't lie, steal, and cheat to succeed. In fact, he says Clinton is counting on that. Larry, on the other hand, is willing to "play in the mud".

"I made a commitment that I could get down there, that I can be the scum of the earth. And I bet that when I get down there, and it was simply a bet, that when I get down there that I can come back. It's a pretty big gamble. I would like to think that I have come back to some form of humanity and some form of honor. But for several years, I was as scummy as them. But I had to be. If you're a goody two-shoes, well, they'll eat you alive.

"I used to say on the air in the early days that I was a

scumbag. I'd admit it. But I'd tell them 'I'm *your* scumbag.' People were willing to say 'He's our scumbag.' The problem is that I can't get the smell off me. I cannot do enough good today to make up. I cannot do enough good stuff to make me forget how scummy I was and how bad I was to people. I literally lived a nightmare for years, hanging around people who were crazy, less than trustworthy, and certainly less than human. But I had to because those were the people Clinton used to do his dirty work. If I hadn't done it, we would have never known what we know now."

To Get His Good Name Back

Larry has done so much to bring forth a mountain of evidence and witnesses that would have gone undiscovered if it were not for his efforts. As a journalist, I have had a number of sources over the years within the law enforcement community at all levels. Often they find themselves participating in activities that are in direct opposition to their own principles. They justify those actions as being necessary "to get the bad guys". It wasn't that easy for Larry. As we spoke further, he explained his concern, which is now a major part of his motivation to succeed.

Larry was extremely close to his father and wanted very much to please him. He was devastated that his actions to expose Bill Clinton had brought a form of dishonor to his family. He was motivated to clear his name and prove to his father that he was telling the truth. The dishonor came as a result of the efforts of his enemies to discredit him. Stories in the press, bogus legal charges that were later dropped, and harassment of anyone who helped him created an environment that impacted everyone in his family.

He described his perceived dishonor. "You're walking downtown and you see people putting the groceries in the bag or whatever. They see you come and you can see them cross the street so they don't have to acknowledge you. People you've known all your life."

Larry says his father read the negative press about him, heard the stories about him, and was disappointed that his son had brought this type of attention to himself. The elder Nichols believed his son was telling the truth about Clinton, but did not believe that it was worth the price Larry and his family had to pay.

He was determined to turn public opinion about him around and "get our good name back. Now you understand why I feel so bad. The only way I could prove that I wasn't what they said was by getting down there among the scum. The only problem was that I ran out of time. I really felt, I guess like we all do, that our parents will live forever. I thought my dad would be here now, when he would see that I did come back from hell, that I was sound, that I was good, that he hadn't made a mistake, and that he could be proud of his boy the way he always was before.

"The problem was, he died. All I could do was promise a dying man that I would get our name back. My daddy died of a broken heart as much as he died of cancer. At the same time I feel like I am such a disappointment to my daughter. Right now she is not going to finish high school. She is going to UCA (University of Central Arkansas), to the college. She doesn't want to attend her senior year. Fortunately, she has the grades to enable her to graduate early. But what kid wants to give up her senior year?"

Helping the Investigations

Obviously, Larry was in a position to personally know things about the Clintons. But certainly not all the things he has reported over the years could possibly come from personal, firsthand experience. His information comes from his own knowledge base and a great deal of detective work. When investigators couldn't get information they needed, they went to Larry and he would somehow get what they couldn't. He has so much evidence that every single congressional, senate, and independent counsel has come to him for his evidence and to get access to the witnesses he has found. In fact, just the fact that the various investigations exist at all can be at least partly credited to Larry. If he had not made his information so public, the pressure and motivation to pursue an investigation may not have taken place. In spite of the fact that 16 different congressmen and senators have most of his evidence and have talked with his witnesses, not one has issued a report or any findings by their investigative committees.

Larry's methods of investigation were certainly not in keeping with high moral standards. He explains that the only time he will lie, steal, cheat is when he is dealing with "the bad guys." If they use those tactics on us, Larry will use those tactics on them. As he said, he is willing to get down in the mud with them. He gave an example of a way he commonly persuaded witnesses to come forward and talk with one of the investigators.

Larry would confront an unwilling witness and say, "Here's the deal. I've now been talking to you. I'm going to let Clinton's people know that I've been talking to you. You are now a dead man. Now, if you cooperate, hey, nobody knows nothin'."

Larry openly admits his methods were questionable, but says, "I've used it a lot. It has netted us a wealth of information that no one would have had otherwise." So how does this fit in with his concern over values? "When you believe as I do that often the absolute of what's right or wrong comes from your conscience, you just know if something's right or wrong. You feel bad when you do wrong and you feel good when you do right. Sometimes you do right and it's hard, but you still feel better. Hell is when you know you are doing wrong and you don't rationalize it away, you know for a fact that you are doing wrong. That's when it's tough to forgive yourself. And that's what I forever carry with me.

"People all the time say, 'You're okay. Don't worry about it. God forgave you.' I'm sure He has, but there's just something about when you do what I've done. It gets to smell on you and you don't ever seem to get it off. That's why I want so much for people to understand. We are in a battle. I have done far too much to myself for people to just cop out and let them win. People owe me that much. I have given more than people ought to give. We need to stop it."

What should the people do? Larry says it's simple. "Often stuff that's simple is not easy. People need to start doing what is right. They need to start doing what's right and we need to enact a law. It's amazing to me, if we enter into a business deal and I take your money and it's your last dollar you have and then you find out I was lying to you to get it, that's a crime.

"How many votes do I have as one person? I get one vote. Then why is it not against the law for politicians to come and lie to me, steal my vote, and not leave me any recourse. Of course, it will never happen. They'll never pass such a law because they're all guilty.

"Some day, and that day has come, some day there will be someone who is so good at lying that he'll make you believe it. One day he will be so good at lying, and will lie so much, that eventually people will not care. That day has come."

I'm Not the Cavalry

Larry is shy about discussing his activities in the Army Special Forces and doesn't like being heaped with compliments, as talk show listeners commonly do. He doesn't put himself in a position to be held up as a leader, although some try to put him in that position. He says, "There are things I can tell you about the Special Forces. There are things that I did in Nicaragua, which, by the way, have been proven, but I won't talk about it."

Larry says the reason for his reluctance is because he is afraid that if the people hear those stories, they will expect him to come in like Rambo and save the country from ruin. He says we are all raised in a "John Wayne mentality" because of movies. We see story after story where the hero, the cavalry, the Jedi Knight, come to the rescue and save everyone.

"I don't want people to have a false hope that the cavalry is going to come riding in at the last minute. You know, I hear a tremendous number of people say we will win in the end. If you look biblically, yeah. I'm doing everything I can to make sure in the end I'm in heaven, but that doesn't mean we're going to win here on earth. We are so close. I mean, we are one midterm election from success or failure. If Bill Clinton gets one house in the midterm election, he will never be brought to justice. Hillary will never be brought to justice. He'll have control of the legislative branch. He does now, really.

"I'm no leader. I'm not leading these people anywhere. They're just craving to follow, but I'm not leading. I'm telling you what I told them. When the Clintons get indicted, then I will have fulfilled my commitment to my dad. Then I will have done all I can do and there'll be no sense in me going any further. I'll hang on and go through whatever process the law goes through, but then I'm done."

Poisoned?

A number of years ago, Larry had an extremely strange experience. He was headed to Dallas to speak to a group anxiously waiting to hear from him. When he got off the plane, the people who came to pick him up were in horror at what they saw. His face was deformed and he was having extreme difficulty breathing.

They took him straight to the emergency ward of a local hospital, where the doctors wanted to admit him as an inpatient immediately. He was rapidly growing worse and all were extremely concerned. Larry told them that if he had to be hospitalized, he wanted to be close to home so he could be near his wife and daughter. He was given a shot and some medication to enable him to make the return journey.

"We calculated the time of the flight plus the time it would take me to drive home. There would only be 30 minutes to spare before the shot would wear off and I'd be in a heap of trouble," Larry explained.

When he arrived at the hospital in Arkansas, he was told that he was within 15 minutes of death. He was suffering from a dangerously high fever, hives all over his body, near respiratory failure, and the equivalent of hives inside his body as well. All three of his histamine systems had broken down at the same time.

During the week he was in the hospital, on more than one occasion a visitor would arrive in his room to find him on the phone being interviewed on a talk show. He had a raging fever and was in terrible pain, but he was granting interviews. Today Larry says he credits the talk shows for saving his life, because it forced him to concentrate hour after hour, keeping his mind active and alert.

"You should have seen me. I looked like the Swamp Thing from the movie. I don't actually remember doing the talk shows, but they tell me I was perfectly coherent." The interviews were just business as usual, with no mention of the difficulty he was having.

Soon after, Larry started to notice a bruise mark that appeared for no reason. It would enlarge over several days, becoming extremely painful. These marks have shown up on many different areas of his body. I have seen his legs, ink black from the knees down, swollen, and extremely painful. The combination of symptoms continue to come and go to this day. For a period of time he's just fine, and then at other times he has another bout with this strange illness.

It was during a time when he was struggling with intense pain from a large black and blue mark covering his chest that he suffered one of the several beatings he has had.

Larry was in his car when a police vehicle pulled him over. Two men dressed in police uniforms approached each side of the car, standing where he could not get their badge numbers. He did notice that they wore the uniforms of policemen assigned to the Weights and Standards Department.

The man on Larry's side of the car reached in the window, pointed to the glove box, and told him to open it because he wanted to see if there was a gun there. As Larry extended his arm, the officer suddenly slammed his elbow into Larry's already painful chest, followed immediately by a backhanded fist to the nose.

The other man began to throw everything from the glove box all over the car while Larry was bleeding profusely and struggling to breathe. The officers made some comments and then returned to their car. Larry was trying to recover his senses when he realized they were flashing their lights and sounding the siren to indicate that he was to drive. Larry began driving slowly, even thought he was barely able to do so, because he realized the men didn't want to place their vehicle in front of his, where he could get a clear view of the license plate.

"It was no surprise," Larry told me, "that some Weights and Standards guys were used as gestapo." Apparently, some of the officers assigned to this particular department were not the normal, police academy-trained law enforcement officers. Apparently, some are hired without the same requirements placed on other law enforcement officers. Larry says that makes it easy to handpick a goon squad.

This incident happened shortly after he had publicly described documents in his possession that showing evidence that Don Tyson, the Tyson Chicken tycoon, was involved in drugs.

When Larry's medical condition flares up, it is always a very painful time for him. The doctors tell him that they can't figure it out. It appears that he has a form of poison in his body, but where it came from is unknown. Blood tests show there is a trace of anthrax in his system, specifically military-grade anthrax. Perhaps it could have come from a natural source, but then again, he could have been purposely poisoned. No one knows for sure. Normally this particular poison is used with the intent to kill—and it normally does.

Family Values

At 47, Larry Nichols is similar to many that age, myself included, who can remember a time when values and morals were at a higher level than they are today. Parents were not afraid to discipline their kids back when we were young. Larry says the lack of parental discipline today is at the core of many of society's troubles. Kids were good back then, he claims, because it hurt to be bad—emotionally. Kids were good because they loved their parents and didn't want to disappoint them. Today's kids have no respect for their parents or anyone else. They could not care less what their parents think of them. Why?

Larry explains, "Today parents say, 'Well, honey, at least he only stole a candy bar. He didn't steal a coke and a candy bar.' Well, when he does steal a candy bar and a coke they say, 'Well, at least he didn't use a gun.' And when he robs and uses a gun, they say, 'At least he didn't kill anyone.' Then comes the time when he robs then kills someone.

"And this is where Clinton and his followers come in. They've learned that people are very vulnerable when they are in pain. You see, the time people are the most vulnerable is when they've lost their job for doing something stupid that they shouldn't have done. That's when Clinton and his gang ride up and say, 'Listen, it wasn't your fault that kid killed somebody. It wasn't his fault. It was society.' And the people are quick to agree because then no one has to take the blame.

"Well, it isn't right. What caused the guy to kill was the fact that when he took the candy bar the first time, his parents

didn't do to him what my parents and your parents did to us."
True.

Today, parents who spank or even yell at their kids are charged with child abuse. No wonder parents are afraid to discipline their kids. No wonder kids are getting away with murder. The majority of kids no longer care about how their actions affect their parents. They just don't care what their parents think of them. And one of the most difficult problems is the number of kids who do not have a stable, traditional, two-parent family. But don't worry. Hillary, that model parent, says it takes a village to raise a child. The problem is, Hillary and her village are really messed up.

Larry is sincere, true to his cause, and very consistent. He has not changed his story since he began his quest, and the information he gives checks out. I've literally spent hundreds of hours listening to recordings of many of those shows, reading archives loaded with news stories. Not once have I been able to catch him changing his story, telling an untruth, exaggerating, or ever taking credit for himself. He consistently, as far back as I can find over numerous years, has been quick to not claim credit or accept accolades. Everything he has told me, and everything I have researched about what he has told others, has been documented. Larry Nichols is for real, and America would do well to pay close attention to this man. He may indeed be our last chance.

2

Damage Control Really Works

Bill Clinton did not invent damage control and political strategies. He simply followed the same strategies used by many others before and since. His claim to fame in the history of the art of politics is that he perfected some basic techniques and uses them over and over again with astonishing success. Those strategies have always worked for him, and he believes they always will. Clinton and his spin team think that the majority of Americans are too dumb to figure out what he is doing. They believe that no one cares enough to even try to figure it out.

Larry Nichols was there from almost the beginning of Clinton's political career. He was one of the people who helped Clinton to learn and perfect the art of lying. Over and over again, Larry and others ran damage control as often as needed to get Clinton elected and keep him in office. Clinton has a system in place that has been perfected from years of repeated use. His methods work so well that he knows exactly what to do with each new scandal, with each new issue to be sold to the people, with each politician to be persuaded, with each new challenge that comes his way.

Larry was with Clinton in Arkansas when they learned those tactics together, and Clinton continues to use the same exact methods today that he perfected as governor. As a result, Larry knows what he will do with each new challenge he faces. When Clinton is lying, Larry can tell. Soon, you will know what Larry knows. When enough people read this book, Clinton's secrets will be known far and wide and he will fall "big time", as Larry likes to say.

Just a Game to Win at Any Cost

Larry remembers to the days when Clinton was Arkansas Attorney General and would bounce around social events telling people his plans to one day be elected president. His goal, according to Larry, was not to be a leader or accomplish something of worth for the country. Bill Clinton's goal was merely to get elected. That was the challenge: play the game and win. Do whatever you have to do, say what you have to say, step on anyone along the way. The goal of the game was to win regardless of the cost.

Each campaign was nothing but a game Clinton loved to play. He never really accomplished much of anything while in office because he spent all his time campaigning for the next election and running damage control. Of course, a major role his damage control squad would play was to create public relations that made him look like he really was doing something of worth. After all, in his mind it was all just a game.

Political strategists and consultants first make big money running campaigns, then they can make even bigger money as advisors once their candidate is in office. Most of them are also just playing the game without any real concern over issues, political philosophies or party affiliation. Dick Morris proved that better than anyone. In a way, they are like a coach in search of the perfect athlete. They work with many, teaching, grooming, and guiding until one day that perfect candidate comes along who can go all the way. Bill Clinton was the candidate of their dreams. He was a fast learner due to his burning desire for power and glory, the looks, the presence, the willingness to compromise his values, and best of all, not only could he lie with a straight face, he could do it with an innocent look that charmed the voters every time.

Larry saw that potential and wanted to be on board Clinton's train. Like the others, he wanted his piece of the pie. He knew if he played his cards right, he would reap great benefits for himself. Back in the '70s, when Clinton would come to On Air Productions, Larry built a relationship with him and bent over backwards to help him in every way that he could. They were both young then, and were both learning. Larry knew that it was important in Arkansas to be accepted by those in power if you ever wanted a chance of getting ahead. Identifying who the good old boys were grooming for the future was critical if you wanted to get some place.

"Bill Clinton was old daddy Fulbright's boy," explains Larry. Senator J. William Fulbright was and is an institution in Arkansas. Because Fulbright put the finger of approval on Clinton, the other good old boys were only too happy to help Clinton learn and progress. They were also happy to help him with their money. If it were not for brothers Jackson and Witt Stephens, along with Don Tyson, Clinton would have never made it to first base. The problem was, he thought when he was first elected governor that he could then make it the rest of the way without them. He learned an important lesson from that mistake.

Clinton was the perfect candidate for the good old boys. He was greedy for power and would do anything, absolutely anything, to win. That was what they needed: someone they could control so they could always get anything they wanted. The powerbrokers need people in office who will work for their best interests, not the best interests of the people. The powerbrokers don't care about party affiliation or a candidate's platform. All they care about is the loyalty of that candidate to them.

Larry was a great contact for young, ambitious Clinton as he began his climb up the political ladder. Larry's clients included all the Arkansas bank owners, which included the Stephens family. The contacts provided by Larry not only helped Clinton fund his campaign for governor, but many of those same people continue to fund his efforts today.

Mr. Ego

However, a young, egotistical, and immature Bill Clinton made a very big mistake the minute he took office as Governor of Arkansas in 1978. His attitude nearly destroyed him. Larry says that, "Clinton would lie. He would cheat. He was dishonest with everyone. When someone would come in, he would agree with whatever they said then turn around and do just the opposite the second they went out the door. When it came to the people who did so much to help him get elected, Clinton just said, 'To hell with them. Now that I'm governor, I don't need them.' He was so arrogant and cocky. He stabbed everyone right in the back."

Arkansas State Police Trooper Larry Patterson, who served on Governor's Security for over six years, confirmed what Larry told me about Clinton's attitude toward the people who helped him get elected. He said, "There were several people who would literally quit their jobs or mortgage their homes to contribute money to his campaign and work in his campaigns—unpaid. They would travel 10–14 hours a day with him to assist him in the campaigns, Then, after the campaign was over, he didn't want to talk to them when they'd call the mansion. He'd say, 'I don't want to talk to that S.O.B. Get him off the phone.' They thought they were close personal friends of his and they called just to visit. He didn't want anything to do with them."

Apparently, according to Larry, Clinton seemed to have a need to show Hillary and her parents that he had achieved some stature. To do that, he purposely stepped on everyone and offended all the people who donated and helped him win. In addition to hurting the powerbrokers who funded his campaign, he also offended the voters. Arkansas has never been considered a wealthy state, but 1980 was particularly challenging economically for many. Clinton raised the cost of registering a car to $25, angering the majority of the people who were living from hand to mouth and couldn't afford what seemed insignificant to Clinton. They were also worried about loss of jobs and entitlements to Vietnamese refugees brought into the state by Governor Clinton.

Arkansas elects its governor every two years. Clinton was given the boot by the voters in 1980 because he lost the support of the powerbrokers and he angered the voters. If he had not slapped the good old boys in the face, they would have helped him win in spite of the fact that he had lost the support of the people. Clinton could have turned public sentiment around and been re-elected. Instead, he was cut down to size with a defeat that taught him an important lesson he would put to good use many years later when he destroyed his own party in 1994. He used what he learned from this experience to bounce back after the devastating midterm election of 1994. What he pulled off with the cooperation of the Republican leadership is a fascinating story we will soon get to.

You Can Buy Anything For Money

The two years between his loss in 1980 and his come back in 1982 may very well have been the most significant two years in the history of this nation, according to Larry. He claims it was during that time that Bill and Hillary Clinton sold their souls to the Devil himself. Larry says that after his defeat, Clinton asked, "What went wrong?" He was told he stabbed Tyson and Stephens in the back.

During those two years, Clinton went back to the powerbrokers and told them what a fool he had been. Larry says Clinton told them he now realized his mistakes and would get it right, telling them that he was young, arrogant, and had made a mistake. Clinton asked them, "'What do I have to do for you if I get re-elected and then become president?'

"That's when deals were made that are now destroying this country," claims Larry. Clinton repaired his associations and this time made the alliances and the pacts that would lead to his run for the presidency. Everyone knew that he was only running for governor to use it as a platform for president.

"He went to the Tysons and the Stephens with his hat in his hand," recounts Larry. "These people were world-class, not just Arkansas, rich. Clinton made sure they realized that he would do absolutely anything they wanted. Anything."

Drugs

During those two years, Clinton was frequently associating with known drug dealer Dan Lasater. Lasater was eventually arrested and convicted on a minor drug charge as part of a plea bargain, and then Clinton pardoned him. The plea got the federal drug trafficking charges reduced to a state charge, giving Clinton the ability to issue the pardon. Larry and others who had been around Clinton early on began staying away when he was around Lasater.

"Many of us here in Arkansas were way behind in terms of things like cocaine. That was scary stuff. We came from a generation that thought the worst thing to do was go behind the barn and sneak a drink of whiskey and have a smoke," he said with a laugh, but was serious. Larry and others knew that one of Clinton's tactics when he got caught doing something wrong was to point the finger of blame at someone else. No one wanted to be around him when he was with Lasater.

Clinton the Liar

The next campaign returned to the tactics of the first one: tell everyone exactly what they want to hear, whether you can deliver or not. Tell them you plan to cut taxes even if you know you will raise them. Clinton lied through his teeth to get elected the very first time he ran, and continues to do so today. He just doesn't know how to tell the truth.

Larry Patterson, who would talk with Clinton in the car after speaking to a group, says, "If we went to five different groups, he'd tell them exactly what it was they wanted to hear. Five groups, five stories. Whatever was politically expedient for the man. I've never seen anyone constantly lie over and over again. I think he deliberately lied to people. We'd get back in the car and he'd say, 'So what do you think, Larry?' And I'd say, 'Well, you didn't tell that guy what you told the other guy an hour ago.' And he'd say, 'F— him, I don't care.' And he didn't care as long as he got that man's vote, support, and political contributions. He'd tell him whatever he wanted to hear."

There does not seem to be much indication that Clinton was motivated by money. Larry says, "You could sit there and wave a million dollars in front of him and it didn't matter. Women and power were what interested him. What kept him in trouble with Hillary is that he would often step over money in the interest of women and power. But Hillary wanted the money too. She wanted him to quit walking off and leaving the money. So when they came back strong in 1982, she decided she would have to take his name. [Prior to that time she went by Hillary Rodham. In 1982 she started calling herself Hillary Rodham Clinton.] That was one thing the people in Arkansas resented. We were not quite that liberated yet. And then the other thing was, she wanted money. That was when it became clear to everyone. She would work at the Rose Law firm. She expected that if you wanted to get to Bill, you came through them. And that's how the money stuff started. It was Hillary that went after the money, not Bill." The money he wanted was our money. Bill Clinton gets his power hunger satisfied by being in control of all the money. That's much better than having money for himself. He has always managed to get everything he needs and wants personally, all paid for without money.

The attention, glory, and perks that come with being a governor and then as president have given Clinton what he loves most. His feelings of inferiority and inadequacy are only overcome as long as he has ultimate power over everyone else. He needs to be in a position of superiority in order to appease his inferiority. Power and lots of approving attention put him on a high.

Clinton turned defeat and rejection into victory in 1982. He turned everything around and learned lessons that have helped him since. He was back in the good graces of the powerbrokers, the money for a winning campaign was now his, the lies spewed forth as needed to win back the voters, and his spin team was getting better all the time. Once the victory was claimed, he never stopped campaigning again. He realized that everything he had learned about getting elected had to continue every day if he was to stay elected. The most critical part of that process was the need for damage control to keep the wolves at bay.

Hillary

The attitude, arrogance, and ego of Bill Clinton could not be matched by anyone else, except Hillary. "Hillary Rodham," explains Larry, "wouldn't even take his name. Hillary totally, totally hated people in Arkansas. She hated being in Arkansas. She hated being around the 'hicks' here. She hated having to be friendly to people that she was intellectually above. She hated being nice to people, including Bill."

Bill and Hillary needed each other to reach their respective goals, so their marriage was one of convenience. Bill Clinton needed Hillary's family because the Rodhams were big outside Arkansas. The Rodhams knew they could use Clinton to help Hillary "become a famous woman who broke the barrier of sex," said Larry, who also explained the sex life of the Clintons. "From day one they had an agreement. It was a swinging relationship." What about Chelsea? "Hillary told her closest friends that they had Chelsea just so they could be a cute couple. It was all just for show."

The American public relates to Chelsea as a teenager, but keep in mind that Chelsea was a very young, impressionable child when Clinton came back from defeat and was re-elected in 1982. Trooper Patterson remembers Chelsea and speaks well of Clinton's relationship with his daughter, but has some telling remarks about Hillary's lack of a relationship with her.

"Hillary would be gone for a week or two weeks at a time," explained Trooper Patterson, "and she'd come back in from her trip, walk by Chelsea, and just pat her on her head. It wasn't a loving, nurturing relationship. One time Chelsea got sick at school and told the teacher to call her daddy because her mother was too busy. He's the governor, but her mother was too busy to care for her sick child."

Chelsea was not alone when it came to a lack of affection from Hillary. The only time the two held hands or showed any sign of affection was in front of the cameras. Behind the scenes they fight like cats and dogs. Although both had a powerful set of lungs and could be heard in frequent verbal battles, Hillary usually came out the victor. Trooper Patterson would dread having to drive with the two of them in the car for any length of time. "It wasn't a loving, close, nurturing, caring relationship," he explained, noting that most people treat their dogs better than the Clintons treat each other.

Patterson was with Bill and Hillary Clinton at the capital, at meetings, in campaigns, traveling, and in the Governor's Mansion. He was with them when no one else was there and they were no longer putting on an act for the public to see. "There was no other person, no other group that had more influence on Bill Clinton than Hillary Clinton. We saw Bill Clinton make decisions and Hillary would see it in the paper the next day and go ballistic, screaming and yelling at him. Before the day was out, he would do a 180-degree turn. He'd change whatever he had said or whatever he was proposing. That happened time and time again," observed Patterson when asked about Hillary's influence on Bill as a leader.

Both Larry and Trooper Patterson report that Hillary would disappear for weeks at a time. No one has offered specifics, but Larry reports that "she fooled around with Vince Foster." He said he doesn't know when the alleged affair began, but that it was interspersed with other affairs, including relationships with women. Larry was quick to add that this was one area where there was no documentary proof of his claim, other than what others have told him. "She ran around with dykes everywhere she went. She would go on the road. Spend weeks. And she would be out with known, you know, lesbians. That's how she got the label that she was a lesbian, from all of the stuff she did."

Womanizing

While Hillary was out fooling around, so was Bill. It was because of the lawsuit of Larry's against him that initially attracted press attention to his womanizing. Although more about this topic will be presented elsewhere, it is interesting to note that Bill took advantage of Chelsea's activities to find women for his encounters, according to the man who helped him with those arrangements.

"Most everybody on Governor's Security," says Trooper Patterson, "will say the one thing that they do give to Bill in his favor was the attention he gave to Chelsea. He took an interest and let her know that he was there. The problem was that when he would go with her to music recitals and other events, he would be there to pick up women."

Patterson told how he actually blocked off a street to prevent Clinton from being caught in the car with a teacher from Chelsea's school, and on a similar occasion with the mother of one of her schoolmates.

Money and Power

Larry's evolving role in Clinton's aspiring plans for greatness was to conduct marketing projects of sorts. These projects were always designed to promote Clinton, make him look good to the voters, and at the same time raise money for some cause. That cause, and the people associated with it, would, of course, feel grateful to Clinton and see to it that significant donations were made at the appropriate time. Larry and others would help these people recognize the appropriate time and how much "appreciation" they should show.

Many people helped raise money for Clinton's campaigns, a simple process that Clinton cleverly controlled. If you wanted a government political appointment with a nice salary and benefits, all you had to do was go out and collect donations for Clinton. Where and how you got the money was up to you, but you better get $50,000 or more because your job might go to the highest donor.

On Air Productions continued to crank out political ads, of course. In addition, Larry would take care of programs such as the "Pepsi Challenge for Better Education," which was actually a project Hillary took charge of. He not only produced the marketing materials and the commercial production, but also approached businesses and got them to donate to the cause along with Pepsi. It was a very successful campaign, with all of the proceeds benefiting Clinton's educational standards program.

All through the '80s, On Air Productions and Larry were involved in projects to help the Clintons look good and keep winning re-election. When a scandal broke, as they often did, Larry would be called in as part of the damage control team because of his skills in marketing and the media.

ADFA

It was in 1987 that Larry decided it was his turn. "I went to Bill and told him that I needed a cushy job. He told me about going to work for the Arkansas Development Finance Authority (ADFA). He actually had the Arkansas Legislature create the job specifically for me. No one had held it before and no one's held it since. There was one problem with the job. They were going to have to put me into some other slot, and I'd have to make $26,000 for a few months until the pay grade was approved for the slot, which would have put me at $40,000 or something.

"That was fine with me, so I got in there and immediately started to see what I could do to promote this agency. I mean I hadn't heard of it, and I was somewhat in the know. I figured if I hadn't heard of it, no one else had. So I started trying to come up with ways to merchandise and market this agency.

"I hadn't been there two weeks until I was told I wasn't there to promote the agency—I was there for damage control. So I started looking to see what the agency was, what damage there was that I was to control. So it didn't take much looking until I realized people were getting multimillion dollar loans without ever having to repay them, people like Tyson and Web Hubbell's father-in-law, Seth Ward, through Park-O-Meter. That was fine with me. As long I did a good job of covering it up, one day I'd get one of those million dollar loans.

"I knew that if they weren't paying these loans back, and the good faith and credit of the state of Arkansas was involved backing these loans, that whoever held some of these bonds they were using to raise the money might sue. So I started looking to see who the bondholders were—there wasn't anybody."

Control Everything

It is important to note here that Clinton knew how to get all his ducks in a row. It is much easier to run damage control if you already control everything. He controlled the media because all his supporters owned the biggest businesses and they could easily control what was disseminated in the news by putting pressure on with their advertising. He controlled the legal system, which was made up of judges whom he appointed and sheriffs who sold their souls to get elected to the same powerbrokers had Clinton sold his soul to. It was a neat little package.

Larry explained that Clinton has very specific rules or models he adheres to and maintains, which guarantees the success of his damage control. "So that's Bill Clinton's first model. He controlled the local media, he controlled the local sheriffs, he controlled the local prosecutors, he controlled the local judges. You see in Arkansas at that time, they have since changed it because we've drawn so much attention to it, it was a one-party state. You couldn't get anything unless you were a Democrat. And in this state to join the Democratic Party and to run and to get its favor, you had to sign a loyalty oath to the party. You had to sell your soul to the devil."

Knowing the controls were in place helped Larry to understand his role in the event that damage control was needed at ADFA. Just like all the other people on the Clinton team, he fully expected to get his share. He was on track—he had been paying his dues and already had been rewarded with a "cushy job". All Larry had to do was more of the same and he was confident one of those ADFA million dollar loans would be his one day.

To Run or Not to Run

It was coming up on another presidential election and everyone knew Clinton wanted to run. There had never been any secret about Clinton's plans, and his supporters, including Larry, were pushing him to run. Gathered in a room waiting to hear from Clinton, the group expected him to declare himself a presidential candidate. Betsy Wright kept the group occupied with a boring speech until, finally, Clinton arrived and announced that he wouldn't run. "We were all pretty let down," says Larry.

"Betsy let us all know that because of what had happened with Gary Hart, the people were not ready for Clinton and all his warts." This was the explanation for the real reason Clinton did not run as planned, according to Larry. Later, many of Clinton's people met with Hart's people. Hart and his supporters had come to the conclusion that he had made a mistake to bow out so quickly. They were convinced that if he had stayed it would have all blown over and he could have won. He needed to play rope-a-dope, says Larry, who knows how well that tactic has worked for Clinton over the years. We'll examine that tactic as well as the others soon.

Predictable Bill

Clinton is extremely predictable because he always follows his own rules and sticks to the strategies that have worked for him in the past. That is why Larry has always been able to detail what Clinton will do in reaction to a given situation when he gets on a talk show. Larry does indeed have many people who call and give him tips, people who are in a position to know and use him to leak information. But even when there is no tip from the inside, he knows Clinton so well that he can predict every move. Despite Larry's accuracy, many will not believe him when he tries to convince them of Clinton's plans.

"Everybody's got his idea of what's going to happen," says

Larry. "Very few people take the time and have the discipline to take their personal thinking out of it and use some logic based on what we know about the way Clinton has done things in the past. I mean, we've got to deal with reality here, and knowing the Clintons as I do, I can tell you reality. Clinton cannot be in a situation today that we did not see in Arkansas. It's bigger, you understand. It was one state, now it's 50. Instead of a state problem it's a national problem—but it's the same. What he did then, he will do now.

"Fortunately for him but unfortunately for us, it works all too often. He is absolutely predictable. One thing that I have said since the first day you ever heard my name, Bill Clinton does the same thing over and over and over again. Bill Clinton has a methodology that once you work something out, once you develop something, then you just keep doing it. And as long as it works, you keep doing it. The only time—the *only* time—you ever deviate from that reality is when something stops working."

Let's take a look at the rules Clinton plays by. According to Larry, these strategies and rules are ironclad, working over and over again. Here's how he described them to me.

1. No Pictures When You're Being Naughty

The number one rule to follow is essential for prevention purposes. If you follow this rule, any necessary damage control will be easier to handle. Never let anyone take pictures. That way, if someone says you did something, they cannot prove it with pictures. It's a simple rule, so simple that Clinton got careless and forgot his own rule. He got a bit too heady with success once and let himself get video taped soliciting donations at White House fund raising events disguised as "coffees". This mistake may prove to be a tough one for Clinton to handle, but then, he is the master of damage control, and if anyone can get out of a jam, he can.

2. Control Everyone

Rule number two is also a prevention step and gives you incredible power if put to work effectively. All you have to do is control all the press, the judges, the prosecutors, the law enforcement agencies, and all the elected officials, regardless of party. Impossible? No, not at all. Clinton did it in Arkansas and has nearly accomplished the same level of control in Washington. You'll find the details of his circle of power discussed throughout this book.

3. My Experts Are Better Than Your Experts

Once you have your circle of power in place, you can easily use this damage control strategy. Here's how Larry explains it:

"If somebody comes up with a sworn affidavit saying that they were with you, then we could come up with ten affidavits from state senators, from state representatives, from judges, saying that you were with us. If they come up with a doctor that says, medically speaking, you have such and such condition, we would come up with 50 doctors that say, medically speaking, you're wrong. When Clinton came up with a budget, if somebody was an economic person and said, 'We've been running the numbers and Clinton's budget doesn't work,' we would get 50 of the top financial minds in the world to say it does. Bottom line, everything boils down to a court of law. And two beats one, three beats one, six beats three, eight beats four, and that's the way you live."

Wow! When most good, law-abiding, conservative, hard-working Christian Americans hear these things, they say, "No, that can't work." What they really mean is that they wouldn't do that themselves, or they have a hard time believing that someone else would do such a thing. Clinton and the people who use these tactics are happy when people think that way because that's what makes it so easy for them to use such dishonest strategies over and over again.

4. Rope-A-Dope

Clinton's people were quick to realize that Gary Hart could have used a technique called "rope-a-dope" to stay in the race and win. That's why they met with Hart's people after the fact to verify that they acknowledged their strategic error.

So what is rope-a-dope? Larry begins by explaining, "If you think about this, you can relate this to current events. Every once in a while, things start to fester up and it really looks bad. Everyone will think the sky is falling, only because they don't know this play. So what you do is a play called rope a dope. You back up, get into the corner, cover yourself up, and let the press and everyone else hit on you. And just let them punch and punch. They will think they are beating the hell out of you. Let them think that. And then sometime within a couple or three or four days, maybe a couple weeks, something will happen to take the media's attention off of you. Remember, the American people have a very short attention span, and the media has an even shorter one.

"So if you start getting in trouble, close up, get in the corner, and let them beat on you. Don't say anything, just adopt that whipped puppy dog look and hang on. Be quiet, let them hit you until something comes along to take the focus off of you. Then we'll just work quietly behind the scenes and we'll make whatever problem you have go away. That's rope-a-dope."

Larry's right. When a fresh scandal hits, the press has a feeding frenzy. They will find every angle, every significant person with an opinion, and they will pounce all over you. When there is a feeding frenzy, the press needs something to feed on. If you have nothing to say, they have nothing to feed on and start looking for a new story. If you say something, the press feeds off what you say and gets others to comment on it. If you say nothing, they run out of story fast.

As soon as the press moves on, the majority of American people move right along with them and forget all about it. At one point, everything seems so bad the critics will say, "the sky is falling. It's all over now." Just a few days of rope-a-dope and the sky doesn't fall after all.

5. Who Are You Going to Believe: Me or Your Lying Eyes?

The next damage control strategy comes straight from Adolph Hitler. Larry claims that Clinton is a big fan of Hitler's political skills, though it's only his political skills Clinton admires. It will not surprise many conservatives to find out that Clinton is really trying to copy many of the strategies used by Hitler. They've been saying that just by comparing characteristics of this country with prewar Germany.

The tactic is called "Who are you going to believe: me or your lying eyes?" The very simple basic rule is easy to put in place. If you tell people a lie often enough, they will come to believe it is the truth. The result will be that soon you will have more and more people repeating your lie as a true statement, which means the remaining people are hearing it more often, only now from additional sources. Sooner or later, everyone will come to believe the lie is the truth.

Some examples in our time: "Gay people are born that way and can never be changed"; "Global warming is a condition that threatens the environment"; "We have to do this to help the children". And here's one we are hearing more and more of lately: "Only trained teachers and counselors know what is best and right to teach children. Parents are not qualified." These are all emotion-based statements that ignore factual data to the contrary and are repeated often by people who want to believe those statements.

The purpose of these examples is not to debate these separate issues here. I point this out simply to get you thinking about the other areas of your life that can be impacted by the spin doctors out there who are trying to mold you into their way of thinking. Learn these strategies and look for them. Clinton did not invent these. He's just one of the best at using them. One day he may be gone, but the consultants who created him already have others in office using these tactics. The same consultants also run special interest campaigns to pass or defeat various measures. Don't let them fool you into believing that an apple is an orange. After all, "Who are you going to believe: me or your lying eyes?"

This is a very simple, basic, frightening method of mind control that spreads like a disease. The more people you can get to repeat your lie, particularly if you can get the press and public figures to repeat it for you, the faster you can get the whole population to accept the lie as absolute fact. No one will ever question it again. Done right, you can convince everyone that an apple is in fact an orange.

"As crazy as that sounds," remarks Larry, "no matter what you see, no matter what you think you see, if repeated time and time again from people who you surmised to be well respected, eventually you will say 'Maybe I didn't see what I saw.' And so there is a play called 'Are you going to believe me or your lying eyes?' And you will be shocked literally at how often and well that works. The key, if there's a trick to that play, is that you have to have the cooperation of the media." And, of course, the media are often the first to be deceived by design of the perpetrators.

6. Let's Have an Investigation

The next strategy requires that you've got your circle of power in place, and that you know how to use "lying eyes" effectively. This is more of an implementation of the strategies, but Clinton used it in Arkansas and uses it now with equal success. It is simply called "investigate." This is one that he uses over and over again to bury everything. Every accusation, every hint of illegality is effectively ended with this tactic.

When I met with Larry and Trooper Patterson together, I asked them to give me an example of this tactic as it was used when Clinton was governor and compare it with a similar event when he became president. Larry began.

"Let's say something would go wrong. Let's say they would have a scandal at the Department of Human Services or the Highway Department. Bill Clinton would call a committee or he'd have the state legislature form a committee to investigate.

"Well, think about that. He or the legislature (which he controlled) would call for a committee. Let's look at today. Here you have Janet Reno. She called for an investigation to look into whether they should appoint a special investigator to look into Bill's activities in the campaign fund raising. Well, think about that."

Patterson pointed out a more specific problem that took place in the Arkansas State Prison regarding abuse of a free food privilege for corrections workers. "The wardens and all the prison employees got free food," he explained. "There was a big abuse about that. Clinton was really big on using the state police to do investigations and to look into all kinds of allegations. Usually those things Tommy Goodwin just covered right up for him."

"Even at that," Larry added, "when they would call for an investigation, the media would just sit there. Clinton would call for an investigation into the state prison system or would ask for a legislative committee to look into it. They were all Clinton's people. In 30, 60, 90 days they would come out with a finding. This finding would state that they had found absolutely no wrongdoing by the governor, or at the prison, or wherever the scandal was.

"Well, what do you expect them to find? But it was always amazing to me that the media would sit there and just go along with that. People would swear they would remember this for the next election. Then the next election Bill Clinton would simply say, 'Look, this has been investigated three different times and each time it comes up with nothing.'

"Now it's the same with Reno," he continued. "It's just

going to come out the same way. What did you expect Reno to say? She said she found no violations by Clinton or Al Gore. Then, a few days later, we find out there are video tapes showing clear evidence that Clinton was raising money in the White House, which is what Reno said he didn't do. That doesn't matter because she still decided not to appoint a special prosecutor. Why? Because they lose control if that happens."

It would seem that Clinton has for the first time broken his number one rule: never permit photographs of something that can be used against you. Although there must have been incompetence on the part of some staff member to allow the tapes to be revealed in the first place, if Clinton had followed his rule, the damage control would have been easier. Still, the Clinton damage control squad will find ways to dispel the problem. They've done it before. After all, who are you going to believe: Clinton or those lying video tapes? Just keep telling people the president wasn't doing anything illegal. Say it enough and everyone will believe it.

7. Dirty Tricks

The next strategy is a sure indicator that a person has sunk to the lowest depths of humanity. It is called "dirty tricks" because that is exactly what it is. This damage control method comes under the general category of "stab them before they stab us". Besides dirty tricks, this category might include threats, intimidation, planting false stories about someone in the press, falsely accusing someone of crimes to impugn their character, black mail, and many other similar slimeball tactics.

Let's ask some questions of ourselves and see if we can come up with some answers. Keep in mind that I am only asking questions and challenging you to figure this out.

Do you remember an incident called Filegate that seems to have just faded away? Do you recall that the press reported that about 900 FBI files on top Republicans were found in the White House? Perhaps you heard reports, as I did, that the actual number of files was somewhere in the neighborhood of 2,500 or so? There are many unanswered questions about that event. There is concern over a lack of action. The most common question asked by my talk show listeners has been "So what?"

Let's explore this a bit and try to answer that question. In other words, why is Filegate even important? Obviously, returning those files was purposeless, since we can assume that the Clinton damage control squad wasn't stupid. If you were one of Clinton's damage control guys, what would you do with each file before giving it back? If you were trying to save Clinton's neck and there were investigations going on that you did not control, would you be worried? Would you try to stop, or at least sabotage, those investigations? What if the information you had in some of those files revealed skeletons in the closets of members of the Republican leadership in particular, as well as on investigative committee members? If those people knew you had that information, would they be anxious for it to not get out and perhaps cooperate with your suggestion that the committee find something else to do—like propose new laws instead of charging people for violating the existing laws?

Think about it realistically. Why is it that every investigation conducted by the Republican majority has gone nowhere? Why did Congressman Jim Leach conduct an investigation that cost the taxpayers millions, allow the testimony to be inaccurate and incomplete, and when it was concluded, not ever issue a single report on the findings?

"I was doing damage control for Clinton long before I was with ADFA," Larry told me. "I helped him for years. I don't want to make out that I was something more important than I was. Clinton had a stash of people like me and we would do things for him. We would save his bacon. We would keep him from getting in trouble.

"I'm not saying that we developed these strategies. They are being used by everyone. The thing that is unique to Clinton is his absolute devotion to the system. He believed in it. We trained him. He believed in it and he stayed with it."

Understanding Clinton's methods of operation helped explain a great deal. It appeared that he had no basic philosophy because he changed his stands on issues so frequently. Larry, however, explained that there was one basic philosophy at the heart of Clinton's desires.

What Clinton Really Believes

"He believed number one, his all time number one favorite politician—his hero—was Adolph Hitler," Larry said, verifying that he had personally heard Clinton say that. "Now, he was not in favor of Hitler killing of the Jews. He simply admired his political tactics, his system.

"Well, the other thing that Clinton believes is that there should be only a handful of rich people, with no middle class. Everybody else ought to be a pauper. Now, when you achieve that, it will be a smooth running machine. People who are paupers are so busy trying to make ends meet that politics is the last thing on their mind. If you can keep them beat down, that is Clinton's utopia, that is what he thinks the world should be. Then you've got it made. No joke, that's what he believes, that's the way he lives. If you look, that's how he manages. Take all the wrapping off and look what Clinton has done in Arkansas. There is virtually no middle class. Whatever middle class exists is controlled. It works for Stephens, for Tyson, and for the state.

"You've just got to understand, Bill Clinton is no joke. He fervently thinks that you must get rid of the middle class. Because if you don't, you have a bunch of people whom you have to deal with. He doesn't want to deal with them."

Back To Drugs

Obviously, Larry Nichols was at one time a trusted member of the Clinton team. Larry backed, supported, and raised money for him. He even helped run his damage control. What happened? Very simply, he drew a line in the sand when it came to drugs. Drugs could not be rationalized by saying "That's politics." Drugs were not something Larry wanted to be around.

Remember that Larry had reached a point where Clinton liked him so much that he actually had a special session of the Arkansas Legislature create a job for him in ADFA. As mentioned previously, Larry discovered that ADFA was giving millions out in loans to Clinton supporters with nothing to be paid back. In a nutshell, Larry discovered there was money laundering involving drug money and Dan Lasater. What I wanted to know was, how did he find out, and what did he do about it? He took me back to the beginning of the story again, when he went to Clinton to ask for a job.

"Clinton said, 'I've got just the place for you to go, the Arkansas Development Finance Authority.' I'd never even heard of it. I had to go over and meet the president, which was Wooten Eppes. I didn't know Eppes from Adam and Eppes didn't know me. I went over there and we visited. I was to report on whether I liked the ADFA or him, or he seemed to like me. Basically more of a 'Do you all think you can get along?' type thing. I said, 'He seems to be an all right kind of guy' and was given the job.

"They didn't have a slot for a marketing director there, so I had my choice. I could wait until they could get to the special legislative session so they could create a position with a starting salary to the tune of $40,000 but it would get me to $60,000 very fast. For a state job in Arkansas, that wasn't bad. Or they would look around and, if I wanted to go on over there, they would take some existing goofball slot and I could move in, although it would be minuscule moneywise. If I needed somewhere to go I could go ahead and move in. It was a deal where, if I spent three months before they got this other done, they would "make it up to me". So I figured, why not? This way it wouldn't look like I was so preferential if I started out at a low level and moved up.

"As it turns out, that has been one of the points that they have tried to use against me by saying he was just a 20 something a year employee. That's true and by the way I don't even fight that. Their position was that he wasn't in a position to know this that or the other. But then, you see, they've got a problem. They went to the legislature and created that position. So why did they do that if I was such an insignificant employee who wasn't in a position to know anything?

"I went to work there in February of 1988 and they had a special session that took place in May. First, they had to create the position, then they had to advertise it, and then I had to get it. So it turns out that had my world not started falling apart, I would have been fully appointed by October. By the way, they acknowledged me in board meetings, where everything I told you is substantiated. That is once again why Clinton and his people simply make the opening volley argument, but don't continue to pursue it.

"Eppes was never there. He would just draw his paycheck and was always gone. That's how I got involved with having to okay the transfer of funds to Clintons travel account to go see women. Eppes was never there and, since we had a weenie of a bean counter, I would have to take care of it. Buddy Young would come to me and say, 'Nichols, we have to get some money for the governor. He wants to go see Liz. You need to tell Bill Wilson to move five or ten grand over to his travel account.' I would tell Wilson this because Eppes was never there.

"On the few times he was there, I got him drunk. I knew that he liked his Absolutes and water. It was only after getting him lit after hours that I got the bottom line on some of the things I needed to know. I would ask him, 'What if nobody pays back these loans?'

"He'd say, 'Don't worry about it.' Then I'd ask, 'Don't you worry about it?' He just said, 'No.' It was while talking to him that I realized they were actually laundering money. It took me two nights of getting him blind staggering drunk when he finally said the words 'clean the money up'. That's when I knew what to look for.

"Unfortunately for Eppes, I came along on his watch and he had to pay for it. About three months after I left, they canned him. He went to work in the Stephens building, where they could keep an eye on him. In his place they put in none other than Bob Nash to take over and to make absolutely sure, that the ADFA was sealed tighter than a drum."

Once Larry knew what was going on at ADFA, he knew what to look for and where to find it. He gathered a great deal of evidence and then decided it was time to confront Clinton. His initial assumption was that Lasater, through his investment brokerage, was taking advantage of Clinton. Larry's intention was to protect him from this threat. The possibility that Clinton was involved didn't occur to him because he never imagined that Clinton would be involved in such a plan. He believed that the damage control needed for the situation was to protect Clinton by dumping Lasater.

Larry told me about the discussion he had with Clinton about his discovery. He said, "So, I went to Clinton on September 13, 1988 and I said, 'Bill, you know, something is going on up there.' And he asked, 'What's the matter?' I said, 'That agency's breaking the law and you've got two weeks to tell the truth or I've got to.' Now, the reality is that when I went in there, I thought Lasater was just using him, using his relationship. But within a split second of being in there, I realized Clinton not only knew about it but was deeply involved. I could kick myself for opening my mouth, but that's what I did."

Here Comes the Damage Control Right Between the Eyes

"He said that he would be going on a trade envoy to Japan in four days. When he got back in a couple weeks he'd make it right. Well, four days later he got on the plane. That same day, I start getting roasted in the media something terrible. Incredible, outlandish things written about me, stating that I was making unauthorized phone calls on state phones. I kept defending and defending the accusations to the point where, in the media's eyes, they had to do something. So, in 1989 I made them (State of Arkansas) sue me. They finally called my attorney and asked what it was going to take to settle. And I'll never forget what my attorney said: 'You don't understand. You're the suer. We're the suee. Normally it's the suer that asks what it's going to take.'

"They signed a motion to the judge that he accepted saying that those phone calls I made weren't personal. So I had in my hands where I'd beaten them. It was close to 17 days later that I introduced my lawsuit, in 1990. I talked about the women, I talked about Whitewater, and I talked about several points of corruption. One of the things I talked about in my lawsuit was the selling influence in the governor's office, so they haven't changed their style much.

"One of the things that happened, the media went big after the womanizing stuff. Of course, Clinton and his cronies got to all of the women and told them to shut up, even Gennifer Flowers. Buddy Young, Chief of Security for Clinton, told them. So immediately the media goes out and talks to the women after they've been told to shut up. In turn, the media lambastes me even more. It was only when Clinton started running for president that the national media came in here. Here's where the magic starts, where it gets tough to believe.

"In comes the national media. I knew Clinton controlled the local media. Why? Because it takes advertising revenue to run a paper. Clinton's people, the Stephens, Tyson, and others, owned the businesses that did 80 percent of the advertising. So with that in their favor, they were able to muscle the local media into not touching this stuff in the 1990 campaign. I mean, here was all of this stuff you know about, the stuff that was written about in the Presidential race, but nobody touched it."

The national media were not interested in the information Larry tried to give them about the evidence of corruption he had discovered but all they wanted to know about was the womanizing. Of course, that played right into Clinton's hand, because he had planned for that already. He wanted it to come out and get it over with. His strategy was set: play rope-a-dope. It worked and they did their stories. Before long, the womanizing was old news. Bill and Hillary told everyone all was well and their marriage was stronger now than ever. End of story—damage control at its finest.

Larry appeared in a video documentary just after Clinton's election to president. He says, "The purpose of the first tape was to let everyone know what I was afraid of. That Bill Clinton would take to Washington this circle of power, the model he had tested in Arkansas. I was afraid he would take it to Washington and turn the nation into Arkansas. And when I saw the Gonzales hearings, I realized I had made a big mistake. I suddenly realized that Clinton didn't have to take it to Washington because it was already there. The corruption was already there. The people there are willing to do anything to keep power. Clinton wasn't in Washington, he was in heaven."

3

Money Laundering

It is difficult to imagine that any current or past president of the United States could be involved in any form of illegal drug running or money laundering. But various accusations to that effect have surrounded Bill Clinton for well over a decade, which he naturally denies. No attempt will be made here to detail the many allegations lodged by various sources over the years. Those are well-documented in other works and are easily accessible to anyone who has a serious interest. It will be my intent to provide information pertaining to that portion of the story which Larry Nichols has involved himself in.

Larry claims that he has not been a participant in personally using drugs with Clinton nor does he claim to have personally observed Clinton using any illegal drug. He does claim to have observed the transportation of drugs in and out of Mena, Arkansas, by plane. He also claims that he has extensive documentary evidence and witnesses sufficient to link Clinton and other notable politicians to a drug smuggling operation.

Larry said he first became concerned about Clinton's possible drug involvement just after he lost reelection for governor in 1980. It was during that time, Dan Lasater and Clinton became friends and were often seen together at parties where drugs were being used. Investigation by the Arkansas State Police found that Lasater was providing free cocaine to many people at various gatherings and parties. Although evidence existed to show that he was a drug dealer and money launderer, a much lesser charge was made resulting in a few months in a luxury style prison followed by a full pardon from Clinton.

Larry and many others have claimed that Lasater, who still owns and operates a bond investment firm, was engaged in drug money laundering. He believes that money laundering involved Clinton and the Arkansas Development Finance Authority (ADFA), where Larry was a Clinton appointee with the assignment to take care of damage control for the agency. It was in that capacity that Larry found evidence to support his claims and has since tirelessly pursued a quest to expose the evidence he claims proves that Clinton is a criminal of the worst possible sort.

Bill Clinton, Life of the Party

"I first noticed him in the early '80s, just after Clinton lost the governorship," described Larry. "It was then that you'd see Lasater pop up. He was a pretty hard runner. Partied a lot. He was a high roller, flashy. Pretty big cheese, you know. Everybody knew he was big into the drugs. He would have parties where that stuff would just flow. You gotta understand, there were a lot of people just like me. I wouldn't have known where to go to get it. So you go to his party and it's the 'cool thing'—everybody's doing it. I wasn't the only one who stayed away from Lasater. Most people knew he was trouble."

Newspaper articles and books about Lasater and Clinton abound. There is no need to rehash old information here, except to point out that Larry is far from being alone in his accusations. In fact, if anything, he has only shed a small light on a rather vast and complicated story of corruption in the very highest places.

"It wasn't until quite a while later," Larry explained, "that I caught on to the drug dealing. I had stopped doing the socializing in the clubs and stuff with Clinton and the boys. You'd be surprised at how much Clinton was there. There's a bunch that have given testimony to Starr about Clinton's drug use. Contrary to rumors, there are no pictures of Clinton doing drugs. Now, there are supposedly pictures of Lasater at a party in Hot Springs, where he supposedly had a plate with cocaine in it with Clinton was standing with his hands on Lasater's shoulders. I would have believed by now that picture would have shown up. Remember, Clinton has a rule about no pictures."

Rumors Abound

Rumors about a video and photographs of Clinton either using drugs or being with people while they were using drugs have circulated for several years, yet none has ever appeared. In May of 1996, reporter Brian Brazil of the newspaper *Free Speech* reported efforts by a retired investigator in Little Rock, Arkansas, to sell videos and photographs showing Clinton using drugs. When he tried to sell the pictures through ads in the paper, *Free Speech* required that the investigator permit them to see the photos before they would run the ad. The man never produced the pictures he claimed to have. He did come up with other video and audio tapes that showed Roger Clinton (Bill's brother) taking drugs and discussing drug trafficking. There were also interviews with women who claim to have had sex with Bill Clinton as well as interviews with journalists, Arkansas state troopers, and even Larry.

After a full investigation, *Free Speech* reported that the retired investigator had lied to them about the tape and photos. They also reported that he tried to extort money from Clinton and the Democratic National Committee. Do the pictures exist? Larry doesn't believe they do. Knowing that Clinton has a strict damage control rule about no pictures, I believe Larry is right.

Sweet Deal for a Drug Dealer

With the help of banker Jackson Stephens, Dan Lasater got into the investment business selling bonds. His investment firm is still in business today and is reported to be the largest such operation outside Wall Street. David Collins and George Locke, who were named in the drug indictment against Lasater, were also involved in the investment firm. Larry reports that the investment firm did not start small and build up. It began large and grew larger still.

At the time, Larry was operating On Air Productions and was actively involved in public relations projects for Clinton. He had just been asked to help raise funds to replace the communication system for the Arkansas State Police because there was no money in the state budget to pay for it.

Larry tells how he put a program together to raise the millions needed for the project under the direction of Col. Tommy Goodwin, then the Director of the Arkansas State Police. The initial sponsor of the program was Wendy's Hamburgers. Customers could "take a bite out of crime" when they bought a hamburger. Each one sold would guarantee a percentage of the sale to the fund for the equipment. Everyone was happy with the plan and Larry was fielding proposals from additional businesses who wanted to get in on what was expected to be an outstanding public relations campaign for all involved.

Suddenly, the entire deal was off. Larry got the bad news from Goodwin in a phone call. Lasater and Clinton had another plan just prior to Lasater's drug indictment. "Goodwin was just on fire," reported Larry of the event. "Lasater was just about to be indicted as the results of an investigation by the state police into his drug deals, and here he is making big money by floating some bonds to get the money for the communications equipment," he explained.

"Clinton goes around to all the legislators, leaning on them, slamming them, and talks them into floating a bond deal. Goodwin was furious. What I was doing would cost the taxpayers nothing. Lasater was about to be indicted and yet Clinton was lacing the deal for the bond through him. The last thing Lasater does before he gets indicted is to do a deal for the state police where he reportedly makes over $700,000!"

Despite a mountain of evidence after an extensive investigation, Lasater was not charged with trafficking in drugs. He was charged with giving cocaine to minor aged girls (14 and 16) in exchange for sexual favors.

Larry claims Lasater received very special treatment. "They even created a new term called 'social distribution' just for him. He makes a plea, along with Locke and Collins and they spend four or five months at the 'Holiday Inn for Criminals.' They got Lasater because they caught Roger Clinton buying and selling. When Roger fingered Lasater as the supplier, everybody figured Lasater was toast. He got out on probation in just a few months, and much to everybody's surprise, Clinton gave him a full pardon.

"It's pretty slick. Clinton's pardon was planned from the get go. They had to plan in advance and convince the feds to let Lasater cop a plea to a state crime instead of a federal crime. He was out in no time, fully pardoned, and back in business under a new name."

According to Larry, when Lasater went to jail, his investment firm was run by Patsy Thomasson. He says she was given full power of attorney by Lasater, which she still has to this day. "Here's the kicker," says Larry, "as a part of what we learned about how Lasater was laundering money. There are three sizes of brokerage firms: small, medium, and large. Lasater, of course, had the largest and best. His firm can do unlimited trades of any size and they do their own internal audits. Guess who was the person in his company who did these audits? Patsy Thomasson. So all of the shady deals that Lasater did that have since been found out—some have even been prosecuted—the person that approved all of it was Patsy Thomasson, who is in the White House today," said Larry, with obvious disgust in his voice.

Go to London for News About America

Most of the press in this country seem to avoid pursuing investigative stories on the scandals of Bill and Hillary Clinton. To find out what has been happening, you need only to read the foreign press. One of the best has been Ambrose Evans-Pritchard of the *London Telegraph*. He reported that a memo obtained from the Drug Enforcement Agency named Patsy Thomasson of Lasater & Co. as a passenger on board private flights with Lasater to Latin America.

When David Watkins was fired as White House Chief of Management (he told a golf magazine that Clinton's highest goal as president was to play 800 rounds of golf and liked using the presidential helicopter for personal golf outings), Thomasson took his place.

When that happened, it was more than Larry could stand. He spent day and night on talk radio shows telling people to call and complain about Thomasson. Along with telling the country about his accusations of money laundering facilitated by Patsy Thomasson, he told listeners that she had never received a security clearance. Of course, as we learn from the revelations in *Unlimited Access* by Gary Aldrich, most of the staff in the White House was not cleared to be there. Larry says the reason so many Clinton staffers could not permit a background check is that they knew they would never pass due to ongoing drug use—and worse.

"We made such a stink," Larry says of his efforts combined with his listeners', "that, just for PR purposes, they were forced to remove her from that capacity."

Drugs in Mena, Arkansas

The rapid growth of drug running in and out of Arkansas can possibly be attributed to Adler Berrigan Seal, more commonly known as Barry Seal. Seal was a major drug runner who cleverly became an informant and operative for the Drug Enforcement Agency. To avoid an indictment against him, he offered to help crack open the Medellín cartel, which he pulled off in a major sting operation. Yet Seal was able to pull off something even more astounding: he continued to smuggle drugs, keeping his own operation going and expanding.

According to reports by Evans-Pritchard, Seal may have the record as the biggest importer of cocaine in American history. His research reveals that Seal and his team brought in at least 36 metric tons of cocaine, 104 tons of marijuana, and 3 tons of heroin. Even though Seal was killed over ten years ago, there is an account at the Cayman Islands branch of the Fuji Bank in Seal's name containing $1,645,433,000.

Seal was using Arkansas as his base. As a result, the early '80s saw a major boom in drug activity in Arkansas. Dan Lasater had come to Arkansas at that same time and was reportedly getting supplied by Seal. All of this is old news. I include this brief description to introduce Larry's comments about Seal.

Larry told me that he didn't know Seal personally but knew of him and heard him talked about. "He was a pretty big mystery man until he died," he explained. "Even though he was being prosecuted and working out the deals with the feds, turning informant and stuff, people here knew very little about him. He was just a rich guy who always carried bags of quarters around. When he died, we found out he was one of the main people bringing the dope in for Lasater.

"On several occasions, while investigating ADFA and trying to find out where the money came from, I found out Seal was bringing huge sums of money in and Lasater was laundering it through his brokerage firm, which was in part using Clinton and ADFA as a vehicle to launder the funds.

"Bill Clinton on several occasions not only looked the other way regarding Lasater and Seal, but we have state police who were working narcotics at the time that testified to Congressman Jim Leach and his people that they had orders and a warrant to arrest Seal. They were called off by Col. Tommy Goodwin and told to leave him alone, to cancel the warrants. When they double checked, Goodwin told them Clinton ordered them to stand down.

"So we have, on a couple of occasions, actual sworn testimony that investigators actually called off investigations into Seal because of Clinton. We have it. We've got the head of the narcotics task force that testified under oath that Clinton had ordered him, through Goodwin, to stand down on the bust of Seal. That was incredibly important information."

Drug trafficking creates a major problem for those in that business. Enormous amounts of money are generated in drug deals that need to be made to look as though it came from legitimate sources. Money laundering is the practice of taking such money and "cleaning it up". In 1985, Bill Clinton created his master piece. ADFA served to be a means to launder drug money and provide "free money" to Clinton's top supporters. The best part, from Clinton's vantage point, was that it was specifically set up by the Arkansas Legislature to keep all of its transactions completely secret.

ADFA and Money Laundering

Part of the reason so many people, including the press, have had difficulty following financial scandals of this nature is because it gets complicated and tough to follow. I asked Larry if he could give a simple explanation to help people get the basic picture of what he believed was happening between ADFA and Dan Lasater.

"What they would do was ADFA would put up a bond, let's say one bond for one dollar. Let's say Paine Webber would come in and say they would underwrite the bond issue. We'll agree that either we sell ten of these bonds by a certain date or we'll buy them ourselves. Then they will go out and try to sell them. If they have any that they have not sold by the closing date, then they literally come in and buy them themselves. Lasater did that to every single bond, buying it for a dollar. He would then turn around and use a straw name, say Dennis Patrick, who, on paper, would buy this bond. The ADFA bond stops at Lasater. That's where it stops trading as far as ADFA is concerned. When it gets there, he would say that Dennis Patrick is going to buy that bond.

"Dennis Patrick is actually the name of one of the straw men he used. He was one that we brought out in which we literally found bonds. Lasater would take a million dollars cash and put it into Dennis Patrick's trading account in the bank. Let's say this million dollars cash was drug money. Tomorrow he would say 'Dennis Patrick's got to sell his bond because he has some financial need.' So then he would say that someone else is buying Dennis Patrick's bond. Then he would take another million dollars worth of drug money, put it into the trading account, and take a certified check from the trading account. You see, he now has a clean million dollars. He put a million dollars into a bank that was dirty money then he took a check from his trading company and put it into Patrick's account. I don't know how to explain it any better than that."

Well, that made sense. Dirty money in, clean money out. No matter how much drug money they had, they could always clean it up with a system like that. The nice part for them was the lack of records being kept by ADFA. Remember, they purposely set it up to protect the private information in the ADFA files. No one could get any information, with the exception of Larry Nichols.

Personal Piggy Bank

With all the drug money and all the people who needed to benefit from the profits, it was also quite handy to have ADFA there giving loans to key people who never needed to make payments on those loans. Plus, the way Larry explained it, the loans not only helped reward Clinton's supporters, the process of getting a loan helped fund his campaign.

Larry said, "The loans are just a good-old-boy system. If you would agree to put $50,000 into Bill Clinton's campaign, if you would agree to write Lindsey Jennings $50,000 to structure the loan, if you would pay another $50,000 to the Rose Law firm to do your application, then you could go borrow a million dollars. And, of course, you weren't going to pay it back—nobody ever paid them back. If you were a good buddy, if you were a powerful friend of Bill, you would go in and you make these loans. They would put money in and finance his campaign. They just had a piggy bank right there at ADFA.

"Clinton would apparently say, 'Hey, you get me elected and I'll give you two million to get your company where you want to go.' It was easy to do because it was funded with drug money and nobody had access to the records. You can't go up to ADFA and see the payment record on anything. Even Kenneth Starr couldn't. When they set up ADFA, they said that if people could come in and look at the records, then they could learn about your private business, thereby gaining an unfair competitive advantage, because they could look into your personal finances through ADFA. So when they set that up, they made sure nobody could get anything. You cannot find one record because that's the way it was chartered and set up."

Did Clinton Launder Drug Money?

Let's assume for a moment that all the accusations about illegal drug running on a massive scale in Arkansas are correct, and those accusations come from many more people than just Larry. According to him, Lasater was and is a big part of it. But what about Clinton?

"Never have I ever said Bill Clinton was laundering one bucket of dope. He hasn't laundered one penny of money. Not Bill Clinton. What I can prove is that not only did he know Lasater and the others were doing it, but he also blocked investigations to stop people from stopping them from doing it."

So if we assume that what Larry and others are saying is true about what went on at Mena in the '80s, and if we assume that Lasater was involved and Bill Clinton knew about it and helped cover it up, and since we know nothing was ever done about all this, made me ask Larry an obvious question: What is happening now?

"Why, if you believe it went on in the mid '80s, don't you think it would be bigger than ever?" he asked me rhetorically. "The man that facilitated the operation was Bill Clinton. He is now the president of the United States. So why would anybody think that the drug problem in Mena has stopped?

"The first day Clinton takes office, he shuts down and fires every federal prosecutor. They weren't his loyal people so he fired every single one of them. Then you find out, and it makes sense as to why the first day he takes office he also shuts down the AWACS plane that was patrolling our southern border picking up planes that were bringing in dope. Now you know why, in his first day in office, Bill Clinton stopped our drug interdiction policy. Now, you understand, he is facilitating the drugs to come in bigger than ever. I know you're deceived a bit about the drug raids you hear about periodically. You hear from time to time about the biggest drug bust in history was made in such and such a place, and people say, 'Golly, that doesn't make sense.' It does if you understand that Clinton is helping his friends to eliminate the competition."

Larry went on to explain his claims. "Bill Clinton is using our Drug Enforcement Agency to eliminate the competition: all the drug runners who aren't a part of the drug ring that he facilitates. They're using our police, our government, to tend to their own drug wars. It is the slickest thing you've ever seen. The old slight of hand.

"Understand that Clinton is not the brilliant crook. It's just that he is following orders. If you're the brilliant master mind, you say, 'With all our money, for us to be successful hauling dope we need to have somebody to run the operations.' That's where people like Lasater come in. You have to have people who are willing to kill people who get in the way. That's where the mysterious deaths start occurring. The *Wall Street Journal* said it better than I ever could in one of their editorials. They wrote, 'Why are people surprised about mysterious deaths in Arkansas? Because it has long since been known that when you have drugs and you have money laundering you have a third part of it, which is people being killed.' They are right. In Arkansas, you have drugs and money laundering, so you should suspect that you would have the third element."

Organized Crime

The combination Larry was talking about could mean only one thing: organized crime. Was he trying to tell me that Clinton was either part of or working with organized crime members? Was that to whom Larry claimed he "sold his soul" after he lost the election back in 1980? How could anyone get away with such a massive undertaking?

Larry was quick to explain. "If you're that brain trust at the heart of this kind of drug operation, you say, 'Let's buy us some politicians. Let's buy us some congressmen. Let's buy us some senators.' And then, if you're real good and patient, as are the Indonesians for example, you just keep trying and you just keep trying. Some day, if you're real good and patient, someday you can place one of your people in as president. And that's where we are today."

Larry adamantly insists that Clinton was groomed and brought up the political ladder by the Arkansas good-old-boys. He claims they own him and he does their bidding. He suspects that at least some of the control of Clinton comes from an organized crime group called the Dixie Mafia.

"I don't know who is in charge of the Dixie Mafia," said Larry, "but you can ask anybody you know in the FBI. They will tell you that everybody's heard of the New York-Chicago gangland mobster. They will tell you that the Dixie Mafia is far more dangerous because they buy up local politicians, sheriffs, prosecutors, and judges." If the Dixie Mafia is involved, then Larry says the problem our country faces may never be solved.

Most Americans find it hard to believe that enough politicians could be bought off to facilitate the kind of drug operation Larry has described. After all, he was claiming that the president cleared the way for drugs to be flown into the country without hindrance from law enforcement.

"The right people were not put in place over night," he explained. "They were groomed over a long period of time, just as Clinton was. In small southern states like Arkansas, it's very hard to get money to run for office. Money wins campaigns, but the people are all broke.

"Imagine, in southern states, you can come in with relatively small sums of money and you can start at the bottom. You can fund the county judge then the county sheriff. You can fund the mayor. Keep doing that in each little county and town and pretty soon you control everything—*everything*. I mean, people can move freely, you can do something very terrible. But guess what? If you control the sheriff, if you control the coroner, then it's ruled a suicide if someone dies, and no investigation takes place. And, if the suicides are starting to look suspicious, you can get together with all the legislators who, by now, you control. You can get the governor, whose name is Bill Clinton, to call a special session and pass a law that says if a coroner rules a death a suicide, there will be no autopsy."

Larry also explained that in many states a coroner is an appointed official who doesn't have to be a doctor or have any medical training. It is amazing what can be done when a politician has sold his soul. Larry's explanation of a progressive effort over the years to take drug money and help fund campaigns made sense to me. With billions of dollars at their disposal, drug kingpins could easily gain that type of control. The thought that they might control the White House and members of Congress, however, is most disturbing. If what Larry claims is true, they do.

"That's what you can do when you control every aspect of government in a small pond. That's organized crime," claims Larry. "Ask the FBI. The kingpins are absolutely ruthless and unpredictable. They kill people, and nobody can do anything. That's who's running your government right now. Now you know why I fight. Now you know why I can be afraid of being arrested."

Heads Up

At the time Larry was telling me these things, he was about to go into hiding. He had received a tip that he would be arrested on a Friday and taken to the county jail on bogus charges. He was warned that he would not live through the weekend if he ended up in jail. For several weeks he was constantly having to take special precautions to protect himself. What a sorry state of affairs when a person is afraid of law enforcement. I asked him why he didn't ask Kenneth Starr for protection and he just laughed and said he didn't know who to trust.

"I've been beat up six or seven times. Hell, one time in Little Rock when I was beaten up, the deputy who came to make the report said, 'If my name was Nichols, I'd watch my back.' I have scars from some of these beatings. Most of the time it's just simple stuff, crack a rib here just enough to make you hurt. Most of the time it's to make a point. You know, to let you know they can get to you anytime they want to. It's to let you know that you're in trouble. "So, you just take the beatings and you go on," he explained, saying that his enemies would challenge whether he has been beaten.

He tried to illustrate how they will use damage control to make him look bad. "The scars are here, the medical reports are here, but you can bet your bottom dollar that in each case the police reports have long since disappeared. And I've had people witness it. And still that doesn't bother them because what's someone going say—'Prove it.' I've got someone who saw it. 'We've got ten who say it didn't happen.' I saw what I saw. 'We don't care. We got a state senator, we got this, that, and the other.' No matter what I say, they've got 20 who say different. Then that's where smearing your character comes in. 'Are you going to believe somebody like Nichols?' It's all so sinister. I know the damage control they will use. They do it every time. It works because the press and the public buy into it."

Larry is very clear and very emphatic that he is not naive enough to believe he can change any of what he describes. His goal is to expose the Clintons and have them brought to justice, at least in the minds of the public if not actually in the courts. He knows the evil he describes runs far and wide and will not be stopped by him.

The Dixie Mafia is not some figment of Larry's imagination. A reference book entitled *Gangs USA* has an entry for the Dixie Mafia, calling it one of the largest, most deadly gangs in the country. It also points out that it is a rather "informal association of white gangsters" and that it is one of the least known gangs by the general public. According to the book, the gang had its beginnings in bank robberies and interstate theft. As it evolved, the members began using their profits to buy public officials through campaign funding. It wasn't long before the Dixie Mafia moved to drug dealing, which brought money laundering and contract murders. Maybe Larry is right about his suspicions. It appears that the Dixie Mafia has the best damage control methods of all, and that is why they are so obscure and never get caught.

So what is happening in Arkansas today? Are drugs still being run in and out of Mena? Is money still being laundered through bonds that no one owns at ADFA? Are people still getting free loans they don't have to qualify for and don't have to pay back? Larry says we'd be crazy to think it has stopped, and in fact adds a new chapter to the story:

The New Mena

"About two years ago, I started getting calls from people in the north central part of the state. They were so scared they were calling from pay phones. They wanted to know if I knew what was going on around Clinton and Leslie, Arkansas. When I told them I had no idea, they said there is a company called Oxley Timber. Apparently they were coming in and they were buying 800- and 1200-acre tracts of land. They came in with brand new equipment, tree pinchers. You know, million dollar rigs. They were coming in and cutting them clean down to the dirt.

"No one could figure out what they were doing because they were hauling these trees past the mills that were right there around where they were cutting them. They were hauling them down to Pine Bluff, which was many, many miles away—too many miles to be profitable.

"They told me that people would be out hunting in and around this property and they would see people in camouflaged uniforms and hear and see planes flying over low at night with their lights off. Sounded very much like the thing going on around Mena, almost exactly. They said I'll never believe who Oxley Timber is.

"By the way, it was like the old land grabs. They were squeezing people, telling them that if they knew what was good for them, they would sell. They were paying cash, taking quit claim deeds to the property. They told me Oxley Timber's corporate address was the same address as the Rose Law firm. But get this: the owner is apparently Dan Lasater. So maybe this is why people in the know around here are saying Lasater is hauling more dope in today than in the days around Mena. There are people who tell me they are observing this today."

It is not unusual for people to call Larry with information of all kinds. When someone wants to make some information known, often they have no idea who they can trust. The one person everyone knows is not a part of the Clinton circle of power is Larry Nichols. He explained that he receives calls from people he has never even met who want to give him information and documents. Larry says they often do it to avoid being charged as an accessory. By giving information they know of to someone else, they are avoiding that charge. They come to him because they have confidence that he is not going to tell Clinton what they have done.

The Creation of ADFA

So in our process of learning about damage control methods, one that obviously works well is to gain control of elected officials through campaign funding and fear. When organized crime, for example, controls the judges, law enforcement, and lawmakers, it can do anything it wishes.

When Clinton created ADFA in 1985, you can be certain it was not his brain child. He was more than likely just carrying out orders. It certainly was to his advantage. The authorizing legislation was drawn up by the man who holds all the keys to bring success to the Starr investigation: Mr. Webster Hubbell, former assistant U.S. Attorney General. At that time he was with the Rose Law firm.

As a former legislator, I am amazed that the Arkansas Legislature had enough of its members who were either totally blind or completely corrupt to allow the creation of ADFA with absolutely no oversight or accountability. ADFA has issued more than $1.5 billion of the bonds with no records kept, or at least none that can be obtained. ADFA claims to not know who purchased those bonds or where the money went.

Fifty Million Dollars

Evans-Pritchard, who I consider to be one of the finest investigative journalists in the world, reported that in December 1988 ADFA wired $50 million to the Fuji Bank in the Cayman Islands. The Caymans are famous for secret bank accounts. There has never been an explanation nor has the money been returned. Other news reports have also been published claiming there is an account in that same bank intended for Bill Clinton which contains $50 million, even though the name on the account is reportedly Chelsea Jefferson. Keep in mind that Clinton received a salary of approximately $35,000 a year in his last term as governor.

Anyone who acts surprised that Clinton and other politicians in Washington could accept money from foreign sources in exchange for favors to those countries needs only to see where it all began. Once you see that this is just a natural escalation from years ago when, as Larry says, "Clinton sold his soul to the Devil," when he went with hat in hand to Stephens and Tyson agreeing to do their bidding if only they would back him and give him another chance.

Once you know the motivations of politicians, once you know to whom they owe their loyalty, does it help to understand why they vote on issues the way they do? Does it make sense that they will clearly vote contrary to the obvious wishes of the people they represent? Can you understand why they will do something that is not in the best interest of the people? They don't care what you or I think. They will run damage control to make us think they are doing the right thing, but now we can see through those tactics and they won't get away with it any longer.

4

On Sex and Clinton

Bill Clinton was never concerned about being caught having a sexual encounter with any woman to whom he was not married. In fact, he actually wanted it to come out and had his damage control planned in advance. He wanted it out so he could get it over with and move on. It was Larry Nichols who first made Clinton's sex life public through a lawsuit he filed against Governor Clinton in an effort to protect himself and to clear his name.

"I was seriously just trying to stay alive," claims Larry. "The best way that I knew to do that was to show how Clinton had used the state police to go see women. I wanted to show that he had used state vehicles and state employees."

The moral questions involved were not the point of Larry's efforts, and in reality he explained to me that he was just using the women as a means to expose the other corruption he had discovered. Larry wasn't the only one who wanted to expose Clinton's affairs with women.

"There was an election going on in 1990 between Clinton and Sheffield Nelson, and so there were people that wanted to take the girlie stuff from my suit and make something out of it. It just kept getting bigger and bigger as a story locally," he explained.

As mentioned previously, Clinton's strategists had met with Gary Hart's people and had come to the conclusion that Clinton would use rope-a-dope when the story broke nationally. Larry knew about the meeting and was trying not to play into their hand, but ultimately that is exactly what he did. When Clinton announced he would run for president, Larry was counting on the national press coming to town and airing Clinton's sexual exploits all over the national headlines. He also expected the national press would look further and publish stories about the corruption he had uncovered. Larry knew the local press was controlled by Clinton but expected the national press to be beyond his reach. He was wrong.

Just What They Wanted

The national press jumped all over the story, and Clinton was ready. He and Hillary made their appearance before the cameras and told the nation they loved each other and their marriage was stronger than ever before. From then on, they went to rope-a-dope and just let the press and public say whatever they wanted. Their strategy worked, as they got rapid national name awareness and a great deal of empathy from a large segment of the American public. Clinton and his strategists believed that the majority of Americans had at one time been unfaithful and would empathize with Bill and Hillary. The strategy paid off and the results gave license to Clinton to continue his unfaithfulness unabated.

In effect, Larry's lawsuit against Clinton actually helped

Clinton's damage control strategy, and Larry agrees. "Imagine me seeing my stuff helping Clinton. The womanizing part of it was brought out to show how he used state funds, used the office of governor, to get women." No one gave that aspect of Larry's suit more than a passing thought. A feeding frenzy was under way and the media wanted the sex story, not corruption. Sex sells papers and boosts TV news show ratings.

"The media was all over Clinton, this little hay seed, this little nobody, this guy who couldn't keep his britches on," Larry related, complaining of the side show aspect and attention to what he considered the wrong focus. Clinton seemed to benefit from the attention rather than be hurt by it. Larry was depicted in the press as the bad guy and Clinton was depicted as the victim, all due to Clinton damage control.

At that time, the women involved were much too scared to talk to the press. The troopers weren't talking yet. Larry stood alone, facing a barrage of attacks from Clinton's damage control squad aimed at discrediting him. That strategy paid off for Clinton. The general public was fooled but those who knew about Clinton's sordid background were not. Numerous people who had evidence or who were a witness to some activity of Clinton began to make themselves known to Larry as a result of seeing news articles about him. Even though the press was generally negative towards Larry, it had the benefit of helping him to find people who could help him. These are people who may not have come forward otherwise.

Larry Strikes Back

It is surprising how many people have initiated contact with Larry by putting a note in his mailbox or leaving some key evidence there for him. In fact, there was one instance when key evidence was returned to Larry that had been submitted by someone else. Steven Edwards, a tabloid journalist, left a note for Larry that read: *I think there's more to you than meets the eye. Can we meet?*

A meeting was arranged at a local waffle house and Larry told him the entire story. He came prepared with a bargaining chip. He knew what a tabloid journalist wanted—sex. He offered to get him Gennifer Flowers on the condition that the reporter would do a straight story on everything Larry had found, not just the sex scandal. Larry didn't actually make the arrangements to get anyone to talk. Instead, he guided the strategy used by the tabloid which ultimately got them what they wanted. Larry sent the reporter to both Flowers and Liz Ward.

Larry knew the local press so well he could predict their reactions to just about anything. He decided to use that to his favor and set up his own damage control, using Steven Edwards and his tabloid newspaper. They wanted to pay Larry for his story and he wouldn't take it, even though this was right at the time he was losing his home. Flowers reportedly received $100,000 and Ward got $250,000. Larry got his story in print and they helped him set a trap for the local press to play into. He explained what happened.

"We would set a trap using Bill Simons, the Associated Press bureau chief here. They agreed to run my story first, and they agreed to be honest. I told them, 'All you owe me is to be honest. If I'm lying, roast me and destroy me. If I'm telling the truth, just print the truth.' You know, the same thing I've told you. Believe it or not, they did a very worthy job with my story. They did a good job of researching. It wasn't the slop and trash you would have figured in a tabloid.

"I explained how they could get the maximum publicity and focus on their story of the women. I knew that of all the local reporters, it would be Bill Simons of the Associated Press who would react nationally when my story came out. I knew what he'd do. He'd say I made it all up.'

"It worked just like I figured. My story broke and guess what? Simons puts out a story on the AP nationally that said I was wrong. He said he had personally investigated everything I was saying and that it was totally not true. He claimed he had checked personally with all the women I named. He specifically named Gennifer Flowers, who he claims told him everything I said was trash."

Edwards had agreed to hold his story on the women until the reaction came to Larry's story. Once the AP story went out, Edwards published his story right on cue. Both Flowers and Ward told everything, and Larry was able to gain some vindication. In the story, Flowers claimed her relationship with Clinton was a 12-year love affair. Larry remarked, "Of course, everyone here knew that Bill Clinton doesn't love anybody. It was a squeeze-for-sex relationship, not a romance."

The Press Likes Sex, Not Corruption

That victory was soon deflated because the next part of Larry's plan did not work the way he expected. He thought the national press would now want to dig deeper and get to the bottom of all the Clinton dirt. He was wrong.

"I figured once that was out there, they would start looking tighter at Clinton and what was wrong with him. Then we'd get the rest of it out. I really thought they would start looking from the proper perspective. I didn't care who Clinton slept with. That's his business. What I did mind, the whole intent of my lawsuit, was that he was using state policemen on duty to hustle for him. He was using state policemen on duty to stand guard over him. And, of course, that's illegal; you can't do that in Arkansas. The national media didn't get involved in all this other stuff. They were just after the cutesy, girlie, sex stuff."

After all that has been said thus far about Clinton's circle of power in Arkansas, it may be a surprise to hear that Larry was able to find one attorney in Arkansas who wasn't loyal to Clinton. Gary Johnson was not only a good attorney for Larry, he just happened to have an important piece of evidence for Larry's lawsuit.

Johnson lived at the end of the hall, right by Flowers' apartment. At one time there had been some vandalism there, so Johnson installed a security system with a video camera and recorder. Instead of catching vandals, his video camera caught Clinton going in and out of her apartment on more than one occasion. Clinton has denied everything, so Johnson and Larry realized the video tapes would provide the proof they needed. If they could just prove one major lie, the public might start to believe there were many lies.

Right after Johnson agreed to represent Larry, he started to receive threatening calls warning him not to have anything to do with him. Johnson was preparing to file some motions and move forward with the case. He filed them on a Thursday, and on that Saturday, Larry found him left for dead in his apartment. It was not a very pretty sight.

"Three short-haired white guys came in and asked him for the videos. When he said no, they broke his elbow. Then when he said no again, they broke his other elbow. And they proceeded to break his collar bone, and rupture his spleen and gall bladder. They did him in something terrible. He shut down his law office and left town. He went to live up with his mother and goes two or three times to the mental institution a week to this day. It scared him to death. They ripped him from stem to stern and he still has the scars. Of course, he gave them the tapes, but he wished he had given them to the guys before they messed him up."

Let's Make a Deal

Larry had no choice—he had to drop his lawsuit. He called Buddy Young, Chief of Security, and told him he wanted to meet with Clinton. Things started happening fast. Larry was picked up and brought to David Watkins' office.

"They had all of these statements they wanted me to sign, recanting and taking back what I said about the women. I refused to do it," said Larry. Several times they offered money but he wouldn't take it. "I told them I would say that it's over, but that's all. I even said I'd apologize to the women for having to draw them into it."

Larry described a childish debate in which Watkins said of the agreement they were trying to draft, "You've got four lines we've agreed to. Now give Clinton two lines that he wants." Larry wouldn't give in to Watkins' effort to satisfy Clinton's ego. Eventually they signed an agreement that would end Larry's suit, and hopefully, Larry thought, call off the damage control attacks on him by Clinton's people.

Part of the agreement was that Larry would get a personal meeting with Clinton. He wanted the satisfaction of telling Clinton to his face exactly what he thought of him. Despite the agreement in Watkins' office, nothing happened. The meeting just didn't look like it would ever happen unless Larry took some action.

"It was right before the primary," he told me. "It had been going on and on and I hadn't had a meeting with Clinton. So I told Buddy, 'Either I get my meeting with Clinton or I'm going to come back out and screw him up and he won't win the primary.' So finally they got me with Clinton.

"Bill hit me with this condescending attitude. 'I didn't know they did this,' he said. 'I'll tell you what I'll do. I want to start an investigation. If we find you're telling the truth, I'll order them to make restitution.' He'll say anything so you'll walk out of there saying he's a good guy. He just does it. He can't help himself."

We learned earlier about this damage control technique. Time and time again, Clinton would get into trouble then appoint people loyal to him to investigate and ultimately clear him. In addition to clearing himself of suspicion, Clinton knew that his investigations could be used to stop others from digging deeper while they wait for the results. He also knew that he could drag out those investigations for any length of time needed, which would give the issue time to fade away in the press. It was one simple tactic that could have many benefits for Clinton.

Larry went on to explain that "Buddy Young was assigned to work with me. Time passed on, and low and behold he found that everything I said was true! They were making loans to people who didn't qualify. They were running shabby books, there were monies up there of unknown origin. Buddy actually called my wife and said, 'This nightmare's over for y'all.' He invited me to a meeting to get everything settled."

Larry was astonished. It actually appeared that he was going to win his battle. He was led to believe that arrangements would be made for him to receive the promised restitution. He met with Bill Pledger, the Finance Administration Officer, Bill Bowen, and Buddy Young. Larry was astonished when they told him that they were in agreement that everything was true, but there would be no restitution of lost wages. They told him there was no mechanism in place that would permit such a payment.

By this time, Clinton had been elected president but had not yet taken office. At one point he was present in the room for part of this meeting. Larry told them if this was the way they wanted to play, he would start everything all over again. He told Clinton and all present, "One day when everyone in the world knows who you are, and I'll see that they do, you're going to fall and I'm going to plant an American flag on the steps of the capitol and you're going to be out of there. There are two ways this can end. Either you tell the truth or kill me."

Never Kick a Man Who's Down—He Might Get Up

So once again, Larry locked horns with Clinton, only now he was president of the United States. Clinton's team had made a calculated play to try to silence Larry, but it didn't work. All they succeeded in doing was motivating him to work even harder.

Right about that time, Larry got some news that hit hard. He found out his father had terminal cancer. "That really took the wind out of my sails," he recalled. "I just couldn't do anything. It just broke my heart. I knew we were all going to die, but for him to die being so ashamed of me. I mean, I knew Daddy wasn't ashamed of me, but I was ashamed of me. I just wanted to get the truth printed about Clinton. I worked hard at it. Part of the problem is when people say, 'Larry, you're such a good guy.' I can't let them say that. Remember when I told you about the bonds? It didn't bother me, because I figured one day I'd get mine. It would have bothered a good man."

Like all of us, Larry has done some things he's not very proud of. However, unlike many people in the world today, Larry has acknowledged his errors. He truly feels remorse and sorrow for what he has done wrong. He has expressed his sorrow publicly and has repented by not engaging in those same errors again. In addition he has gone the extra mile to be a better person by improving his character and integrity. He has gone from someone who would lie, cheat, or steal for personal gain to someone with zero tolerance for any form of dishonesty. Larry was once a very selfish man, but now he puts his own needs dead last while he puts the needs of his country and its future first. From what I have seen, he has repented in a way that should be acceptable to both God and man. If he was down in the mud with the scum of the earth, he has certainly risen far above it.

So the battle was back on and it continues to this day. Larry has many amazing skills, one of which is his ability to retrieve information. As we were discussing the women in Clinton's life, it occurred to me that I wanted to know how on earth he knew so much about so many of them. He told me of his many days literally keeping Clinton under total surveillance. In other words, he followed him.

Distinguishing Characteristics

There has been a great deal of speculation in the press and on talk shows particularly (mine included) about the comments from Paula Jones that she can in some way describe something unique about Clinton's genitalia. On my own talk show, I had a caller who suggested that when Clinton injured his knee, he had some additional surgery by a plastic surgeon. I told Larry about the caller and asked if he could fill me in on the truth.

He told me the story of how he discovered the secret about Clinton's anatomy. Paula Jones has claimed from the beginning that she can identify something distinctive about Clinton to prove that he exposed himself to her and asked her to perform oral sex. Jones has not told Larry what that secret is, but he was able to do some detective work and find out for himself. He had not set out to look for that particular piece of information, but his excellent detective work enabled him to discover it. The secret was not anything I had heard rumored nor anything I had even imagined. Here is his story:

"One of the people I cornered early on, one of the people I had literally seen Clinton with, was this black lady. She was about four foot eight. Now it's going to sound like I'm exaggerating, but I'm not. She was about four foot eight and had, yes, blond hair. She weighed between 250 and 260 pounds. She had one or two, I think both front teeth were gold. This is who I caught with Bill Clinton.

"Once he left her, I cornered and queried her. I told her that she had been caught and that all these bad things were going to happen to her. Bless her heart, I lied to her. She panicked. She said, 'Oh, don't cost me my job.' She was the night manager of a McDonalds."

I wanted to know how Larry found Clinton with this woman in the first place. That's when I found out what a good detective he is. The story he tells has been verified by two former state troopers who brought Clinton to see this woman.

"I found her because I was following him. I wanted to track him down, find out what he was up to. Everybody knew all kinds of stuff about Clinton, but nobody had ever been stupid enough, brash enough, dumb enough to follow him. It's one thing for Clinton to do all of these things, but you had better prove it. I've told you the drill. No pictures and all that. So the only way to break the system down would be to follow him and catch some of this stuff.

"Clinton would go out like he was jogging. He would get a block or so away from the governor's mansion and up would pull the governor's limo or a police car. You know, zip up like you see in the movies, slam on the brakes, and everybody'd jump out and hover around him and get him in the back seat. Then they'd drive him over to this black girl's house. He'd go in and tend to business. After thirty minutes or so, he would come out. They would zip him back to within a block of the governor's mansion. He would get out, start jogging in place, take a cup of water, pour it over himself like he was sweating, and jog on in the rest of the way."

As I listened to Larry describe Clinton's midnight escapades, I kept thinking how juvenile it all sounded. Such antics might be expected of a wayward teenager, but to hear of a grown man, a governor, doing such childish maneuvering was both disappointing and astonishing. Issues regarding morality, self-control, and extreme selfishness aside, Clinton's alleged methods to obtain gratification were absolutely immature. When I had the chance to question Trooper Larry Patterson about the frequency of such events, he told me something even more astonishing. The trooper claims that such childish antics were nearly a nightly occurrence when Clinton was in the state.

Larry continued with a description of his interview with the woman. "So I asked her, 'How will I know if other women have been with him? You know, tell me the poop about Clinton.' And that's when she told me he had a very, very small, almost to the point of what you would call deformed, penis. I mean this guy is lacking badly, if you know what I mean. She said he was 'iddy biddy', about two inches. Then, she said he had a fetish—he was just a wild man about oral sex. I mean, he was just crazy. And then she told of a mole, she called it that, but it's actually a birthmark, on the outside of his left buttock. Anyway, that's where I got that. She also told me whether or not he was circumcised, which I have never told anyone. That's something that as long as we don't talk about it and don't let it out, we still have a tie breaker as to whether or not anybody's been with him."

That was the last thing in the world I would have expected to hear. In fact, there's no way I would have ever imagined it. Like everyone else, I expected to hear about a wart, a mole, or some kind of scar or other mark. Obviously that "distinguishing characteristic" was not something that could be eliminated by some clandestine plastic surgery while also repairing an injured knee.

After hearing the woman's story, Larry decided to talk to some psychologists. He wanted to know if such a condition was known to exist. It does. He was told that when this happens to a man it causes some psychological conditions and characteristics. To verify Larry's story, I too spoke to a medical doctor and a clinical psychologist. None of the professionals to whom Larry or I spoke would permit his name to be used in print, which is certainly understandable. Between Larry's efforts and mine, there is no question in my mind that what we learned could be verified by others (unless, of course, Clinton's damage control guys get to them first).

The professionals to whom Larry and I spoke did not, at first, know who we were talking about. They were asked about the condition and the characteristics that would be expected to be found about such a person's behavior. In general, they described a man who has a severe inferiority complex that he learns to hide at an early age. He learns to be an actor, pretending to be the macho, super stud he wishes he really was. To do this, he talks about his sexual prowess and conquests frequently. It is also common that such a person will fantasize about being more well-endowed and indulge in the use of pornographic materials.

Because he is constantly thinking about sex, he has a constant desire for it. The doctors said it would be expected that such a man would only have oral sex, and would want others to know about how frequent and how many women he would have as partners. In other words, being caught only helps him to further the image he is trying to portray to overcome his feeling of inadequacy. The psychologist said to me that because the person with this condition is living in a world of lying to himself and others, he will often extend the lying to everything. He constantly changes his story because he has lost the ability to distinguish between a lie and actual truth. When I told both of these men whom I was actually talking about, they both reacted with comments to the effect that if this condition were factual, much of Clinton's behavior was now more easily understood.

What Larry found out from those he spoke with was similar. He told me that, "As it relates to someone who is truly that small, what happens mentally to them is they feel less than manly. A typical thing for somebody like that is their way to make up for their manhood is to conquer many women. In other words, they have to achieve volume. And, of course, the reason he is so engrossed in oral sex, is that he feels, due to his size, that he can't satisfy women. So that's why he does the oral sex. He thinks that is the way for him. Lo and behold, here we have a guy who has a legitimate mental situation. And it's all true. If you look at it from that perspective, then you realize some of the things he does every day and it makes a little more sense."

The encounter described above was one of many that Larry observed by following Clinton on his nightly rounds.

There is no need to give the specific details of other incidents. But aside from the fact that this was such a regular activity, it is interesting to note the characteristics of the women he seemed to be attracted to for his liaisons. I would have thought, and perhaps others assume the same, that if all the stories were true about his womanizing, Clinton must have been going after the most beautiful women he could find. Larry says that is a false assumption.

"He's got a fetish for black women," he told me, "and he's got a fetish for what you and I would consider to be less attractive women. I think the reason for that, I found out, is that it is easier to get volume. He must have learned early on that beautiful women are hit on a lot and are therefore harder to get. Less than beautiful women are hit on less and those are easier for him to attract. That's why Clinton goes after women you and I would not be attracted to. Because they are easier to get quicker."

Because of all the publicity over quite a period of time, numerous witnesses have contacted Larry on their own. Sometimes it would be one of the women who had been with Clinton, and other times it would be someone who had knowledge of something else regarding the alleged corruption surrounding the Clintons. These people would either meet with him or just send him information they knew would be helpful to him. This process continues to this day. People Larry has never met, who have witnessed something or have some document, continue to call or stop by to see him.

One of the women who met with Larry was Sally Purdue, who had a most amazing story she wanted to tell about sexual encounters and drug use with Clinton. Although her story is not new, it is worthy of note because of what happened to her as a result of going to the press.

Purdue claimed that she and Governor Clinton were having a sexual relationship that also involved the use of cocaine. She told of wild times with Bill Clinton prancing around nude wearing Sally's underwear on his head and playing a saxophone after having used cocaine together. This was not a single event, according to Purdue. She claimed that she was one of Clinton's regular girls.

Apparently Purdue's vivid descriptions to the press hit a nerve somewhere. Larry told me, "Because she was coming forward, while she was up in Missouri working at a college, a Clinton person came and told her that if she didn't quit talking to the media her pretty legs would end up broken. Right after that happened, the window in her car was broken out and there were shotgun shells in the back seat. So she fled. She's gone."

The list of women who know about Clinton's sexual adventures and drug use seems almost endless. It is not my purpose to provide the sordid details of all the encounters here. The tabloids are the place for that. My hope is that we can see a pattern of behavior which should tell us something very basic about our president. It is also significant to note that there are many people who have provided information to the Kenneth Starr investigation, not only about Clinton's personal drug use, but also his involvement with and assistance to drug traffickers. There are people who have come forward and have wisely not gone to the press.

"She's Got That 'Come Hither' Look"

When Clinton wanted to have sex, which was apparently rather frequently, he never did the asking himself. He always had his security officers do it for him. "After all," he may have thought, "that's what hired help is for." He would be at an event and send them out in the crowd. If they ever came back unsuccessful, Larry says "he would literally go crazy because they failed at their mission. And if they failed at their mission, they would have to pull hell duty for a couple of weeks. Of course, hell duty was security for Hillary."

There were ten Arkansas state troopers assigned to

Governor's Security under the command of Buddy Young. For over six years, one of those men was Larry Patterson. I asked him if Clinton made his sexual activity known to him from the start.

"It took two or three months from the time I got on the detail, but yeah. I guess he got to the point where he got to trust me or knew what I was about. He didn't try to hide it anymore from me. On the detail there were five that he trusted. I consider myself one of those that he shared a lot of stuff with and he wasn't afraid to do these things in front of. Some on the detail he would not. He would call me at nine, ten, eleven o'clock when he was going into the mansion at night, and he would ask, 'Larry, who's working midnights tonight?' And that was always a clue as to whether he was going to be out and about doing his thing."

Trooper Patterson said that Clinton had about fifteen to eighteen women that he regularly saw, plus he would have one-night-stands with an unending parade of different women. "This man," he described, "if he wasn't out of town at a meeting, was either with some woman or was chasing a new one all the time. It was a constant thing."

Indeed, Patterson admits to being one of Clinton's best at getting women for him. His willingness, he explained to me, was motivated by fear that he would lose his employment if he did not comply. Clinton would send him out to retrieve sex partners, and he would come through.

He described what often took place, saying, "This was a favorite saying of his. He'd say, 'Larry, the lady out there has that "come hither" look.' Or he'd say, 'She's really coming on strong. I'm going to have to do something about her.' He's the chief executive of the state. He's a big, good-looking guy. He's got a really good personality. So the women flock to him. It was not hard to get them to participate."

Trooper Patterson or other security guards would simply walk up to the woman Clinton had selected and tell them,

"The governor wants to be with you." The women got the message and were usually very willing participants. Usually. Not always, as we have learned from Paula Jones.

Encounters happened everywhere Governor Clinton went. Patterson said Clinton was very supportive of Chelsea's school events and recitals because he considered it a great place to pick up women. One such occasion early in the trooper's assignment was very telling.

"I had blocked the driveway at Chelsea's school so he could meet this lady and spend about 45 minutes with her. He got back in the car and asked, 'How are we going to account for this period of time?' I said, 'Watch this.' I picked up the radio and I reported in. I told the trooper, 'We've been out at a friend's house.' The trooper said, '10-4.' Clinton patted me on the shoulder and said of the trooper who had responded, 'He is my friend. He will lie for me, steal for me, cheat for me, kill for me.' He said, 'You have to do the same to cover for me.'"

Trooper Patterson wasn't about to kill for Clinton, but he was a willing participant in covering up for him. The reason, of course, was fear. The press had criticized him severely because he waited so long to come forward with his claims. Both he and Roger Perry had not been willing to speak out until after Clinton was in Washington.

His explanation to me was understandable. He said, "I had 20 years of my life invested in the department. I was afraid. I knew that if I came out while Bill Clinton was still the seated governor and had he lost the presidential election, he'd still be the governor, you see. I knew if I told my story I was going to be toast. They would find something to fire me for. I was afraid of losing my job. I had a daughter who was still in high school at that time. I know that's probably a real lame excuse. I have some remorse and guilt feelings because I didn't come out early, but I didn't and that's the reason why."

Justification and Gennifer Flowers

During the many long trips in the car with Clinton, Patterson says they spoke openly on many subjects, and Clinton eventually built up a strong trust with him. He shared many personal things with the trooper, one of which was that he claimed that oral sex was not a sin and was not considered adultery if the individuals involved were not married to each other. Patterson asked how he had come to that conclusion and Clinton told him that he had researched it in the Bible and that he had talked to a minister about it. The minister agreed that it was not a sin nor was it adultery.

A college writing instructor I once took a class from at the University of Lowell many years ago made a comment when there was a discussion in class regarding religion. He said, "One man's religion is another man's belly laugh." Well, I make it a habit not to laugh at another man's religion, and in this case it almost makes you want to cry, not laugh. When a person interprets religious principles to justify his own immoral behavior, I feel very sorry for that person. On the one and only occasion when I met Bill Clinton at the White House in 1994, I told him that my family and I prayed for him. If anyone needs our prayers, it is he.

If, as Larry claimed, Clinton preferred generally less attractive women as well as black women, I was a bit confused. You may be wondering, as I did, how that explains the women who did not fit that description. According to Larry, the ones he let be seen with him publicly were good-looking white women. The ones he met in the dead of night were not. Gennifer Flowers is a very good example. I asked Larry what her role was over the years that she and Clinton were seeing each other.

"Gennifer sang in the clubs, cabarets or honky tonks. She also was an up-and-coming TV news reporter when Clinton met her," he explained. "Gennifer was just not that good at singing, but she was the kind of person who would go to bed to get where she needed to go. She was a real name dropper, and, of course, she was really quick to boast that she had been with the governor. What their relationship had evolved into was whenever it got to where Clinton couldn't get anyone else, if it was a situation where Hillary was not around, if he couldn't go out catting, if he couldn't do the things he'd like to do, then they could always count on Gennifer as the main squeeze. That's what role she played, and everyone knew it for years. It wasn't romance."

Those of us in the talk show business receive a report called *Radio and Television Interview Report*. It contains nothing but ads from book authors and publishers who want free publicity through interviews. For three or four months in a row there was an ad offering interviews with Gennifer Flowers about her book. It was obviously planned to be a major release with lots of publicity. I called the publicist each time the report came out, about every two weeks. Each time I requested an interview and each time I was told the book was delayed, and that I should call back. Eventually the book did come out, but no review copies were available and no interviews would be given. Why the change in plans? Had someone influenced her to minimize the impact the book would have?

At that same time, I got an e-mail message from a listener alerting me that Flowers was running a pay–per–use type of live-action pornographic internet site. My purpose in relating this information here is not to promote either the book or the Internet site, and you will note I have purposely not given the name of either. My purpose is to point out that the person who claims to have had a 12-year romantic affair with Clinton is allegedly engaged in high-tech pornography and electronic prostitution. It is also interesting to note that at one time she was planning a large media blitz to promote her book about her relationship with Clinton. What happened to cause that promotion to be canceled? Knowing that Flowers has been motivated by money in the past, is it possible that someone paid her to cancel her plans? These questions remain unanswered because she has not responded to my requests for an interview.

Paula Jones

Paula Jones was certainly the biggest mistake of Bill Clinton's quest for sex. Or would it be more appropriate to lay the blame on State Trooper Danny Fergusson (also named in her suit) for not being more specific when he told Jones that the governor wanted her to come by for a visit? In any case, she has certainly created the damage control challenge of the decade for Clinton.

Larry has had many conversations with Paula and her husband Steve and has provided quite a bit of information and advice to them. Unfortunately for them, they didn't take his initial advice about the lawyers working for them. Larry warned them that there were too many ties between the lawyers and Clinton. But those lawyers are now history and she seems to have her case back on track.

According to Larry, the obvious strategy of Jones is to establish a pattern of behavior by Clinton. In other words, to show that her experience with him was not unique. In fact, such events in the life of Clinton were almost a daily occurrence. To establish this pattern of behavior, her lawyers will use the discovery process to take sworn testimony from 15–17 state troopers. Those troopers, according to Larry Patterson, will not lie under oath. Additionally, there will be a list of women who will be questioned as well, perhaps as many as 30–50, according to Larry.

It's no wonder Clinton's damage control team is working so feverishly to discredit everyone and anyone involved with the case. Obviously, it would be in Clinton's best interest to settle out of court, but Jones seems to have made it clear that she will only do so if a full and complete admission of guilt with an apology is made. Which would be better? Admit guilt, pay the legal fees, and play rope-a-dope until the press finds something else to write about? Or sit by while discovery takes place with a fresh new scandal every day for months?

If what Larry claims to be the distinguishing characteristics of Clinton's anatomy is true, wouldn't it seem logical that it would be too painful an experience for him to go through? Wouldn't it seem logical that he would settle this at all cost rather than go through the ridicule such a disclosure would bring?

Recently we saw Clinton's damage control team, headed by his attorney Robert Bennett, use one of their classic strategies in an effort to diffuse the claims of Jones and discredit her story. They had Clinton's private doctor, Kevin O'Connell, issue a statement to the effect that Clinton's sexual anatomy was of normal size and without unique marks. Clinton has a long history of conducting his own investigations to clear himself from various accusations. No matter how many witnesses someone presents who make a claim about Clinton, he always comes up with his own credentialed witnesses to discredit the claim. This tactic should surprise and fool no one. Unfortunately, it does. That is why he continues to use it.

This is the very reason this book was written: to explain to the American people the devious tactics used by Clinton to deceive them. When the majority of the public is armed with the truth about the Clinton damage control methods, he and his spin doctors will be faced with defeat.

Larry would like to see Jones' suit go to court. He believes a great deal of additional information could be found in discovery that will be of help in pursuing Clinton's other alleged crimes. But he expects Clinton to settle out of court before any of that can happen.

"If he comes out and settles with Paula, if he does it quick, does it slick, and does it smooth, it will be a day's story, maybe two or three days. Here's what's going to happen. The 40 percent of the people who hate Clinton's guts are going to say, 'See, I told you.' And then the 40 percent of the people who love Clinton are going to say, 'He did it for us. He did it for the country. That way he can get on about the nation's business. He didn't admit to anything more than the man in the moon.' And then the 20 percent in the middle are going to say the same thing they always say: 'So what?' That's exactly what they're going to play for."

Because of all the years working for Clinton on damage control, Larry has a good sense for the type of discussion that may be taking place between Clinton and his damage control team in the White House. Larry told me, "If he goes through the discovery route, then every day there's going to be a new scandalous story. That would have an aggregate toll. Then you can see some public sentiment change. So that's why Dickie Morris is going to tell him what I would tell him: 'Bill, let's ace this thing. There are no pictures. Let's come up with a statement. Let's make it as ambiguous as we can pull off with Paula. We'll pay the money to the attorneys. We'll tell them, 'Hey, you all did great, and here's what we're going to do. We'll pay you this bonus. You all work on Paula now and make sure she gives us an angle out.' They've got until Paula and her attorneys start dragging people in under discovery."

That is what Larry told me before Jones fired her attorneys. She did so because they tried to get her to accept an ambiguous, less-than-full apology—as Larry had predicted. They were offered far more money than they asked for—the bonus Larry predicted. He was right in his assessment of what would happen. He knew what Clinton would do, but he forgot to take into account that Jones is very stubborn and will stick with it until she gets what she wants. She is in the driver's seat and Clinton is at her mercy. Just as Larry could not be bought off or frightened away, neither can Paula Jones. She has the determination to stay and fight.

Larry says there are other women waiting in the wings who had similar or worse situations than Jones did. They will testify, and may even pursue action of their own pending the results of the Jones case. Apparently at least two of them have attorneys who are working on ways to have the statute of limitations waived. It will be interesting to see what transpires, at least under discovery.

They key question that Larry first brought to light in his lawsuit was, is it legal for Bill Clinton to use taxpayer-funded resources to satisfy his sexual desires? That question was valid at the time Clinton was governor and it is valid now that he is president. If he was using state money and resources to have sexual encounters with women while he was governor, there is no reason to expect think that the claims made by former FBI Special Agent Gary Aldrich in his book *Unlimited Access* are not true. Aldrich claims that President Clinton is using his secret service agents to arrange sexual partners for him, just as his Arkansas Governor's Security team did back in Arkansas. Is this an appropriate use of taxpayer money?

We must ask ourselves the following question: If everything said about Bill Clinton's sex life is true, what difference does that make when it comes to his being president? Does it matter? Larry thinks it does. I believe it does, and I hope and pray the majority of Americans think it makes a difference. Those of us who do think it makes a difference need to scream loud and long, or in the end it really won't matter. Nothing will happen if grassroots America doesn't stand up and shout, and not cease shouting until justice is served.

5

Clinton's Circle of Power

Prior to the election of Bill Clinton as president, Larry admits his motivation to expose Clinton's crimes was personal retribution. Everything he was doing was directed toward getting even for the way he had been treated by Clinton, and regaining his good name in the community. It wasn't until after the election that he expanded his efforts to "save America from Bill Clinton." Larry knew about Clinton's circle of power in Arkansas and feared he would establish the same type of control in Washington.

While in Arkansas, Clinton established his own little dynasty where he controlled everything and got his own way, according to Larry. He controlled who was in office by controlling who got money to campaign and who didn't. Clinton controlled bureaucracies through appointments to his most loyal supporters. Clinton defined loyal supporters as those who obtained the most donations for his campaign fund. The majority of judges, prosecutors, sheriffs, legislators, county commissioners, and others in elected or appointed positions were dependent on him for their continued existence in that position and feared what would happen if they did not go along. Larry and others claim that Clinton maintains an even greater level of control in Arkansas today.

Trooper Patterson, who protected Clinton's life for over six years, explained to me why he went along with his demands for so long. Patterson was no different than the many others Clinton controlled. He knew that if he did not do as he was asked, he would lose his job and not find another. He had to go along to get along. But Patterson was not alone in these fears. Clinton controlled everyone that way.

And who controls Clinton? Larry points to powerbrokers like the Riadys, Huang, Tyson, and the Stephens. Clinton discovered what would happen when he crossed them in 1980, which resulted in losing their support and the governorship. He learned his lesson. To regain power and move on to become president, Clinton became a loyal, obedient servant—a puppet. It was a great partnership. As long as Clinton did their bidding, he could rule his dynasty.

As Clinton headed off to Washington, Larry knew that he would take his circle of power with him. He would control every appointed office, all the prosecutors, judges, and would eventually the majority of elected officials. He would do it by using the same damage control tactics he had used so successfully in Arkansas. By the time he had his circle of power in place, the people would not have any idea of what had happened. More importantly, the powerbrokers would continue to control him and everyone he controlled.

It was this realization that changed Larry from fighting a personal battle to fighting for a cause. He was now determined to warn the public and nothing would stop him. Every obstacle imaginable was thrown in his way, but he's like the Energizer bunny—he just keeps going, and going, and going.

Clinton is Predictable

Larry says the key to understanding Clinton is understanding his damage control tactics and knowing that he is extremely predictable. He says, "Even when I don't get tipped from the inside, even when people inside the White House who have been there since day one and have been loyal to me since day one, I mean, even when they don't tell me the real poop, often times I don't need to get the tip. I know what he's doing. Clinton cannot be in a situation today that we did not see in Arkansas. It's bigger, you understand. It was one state, and it's now 50. Instead of a state problem, it's a national problem—but it's the same.

"And we have just seen Clinton through incredible parallels," he continued to explain. "We know how he successfully manipulated this that or the other here in Arkansas, therefore we know what he will do now. It works all too often. He is absolutely predictable. One thing that I have said since the first day you ever heard my name: Bill Clinton does the same thing over and over and over again. And to a novice who doesn't understand his methods, the novice keeps saying, 'No way, we're too smart to fall for that.' But it is not true.

Clinton has a methodology that once you work something out, once you develop something, then you just keep doing it. You keep doing it as long as it works. And as long as it works, you keep doing it. The only time you ever deviate from that reality is when something stops working." The problem is, those tactics continue to work for Clinton and others over and over again, and will continue to work until the people recognize what is going on.

Larry believes that his continual effort to teach the people over talk radio about the deception going on will eventually prevail and enough people will stop believing all the damage control tactics by Clinton and others.

These are the main strategies:

1. Never let anyone take pictures when you're doing something wrong;
2. Play rope-a-dope;
3. Are you going to believe me or your lying eyes?;
4. Conduct your own investigations with your own witnesses.

Knowing what Clinton would do in Washington, Larry set out with his plan to warn the country. That plan began by providing information to the print media, it expanded to talk radio, and evolved into video documentaries, which in turn brought him even more requests for talk show interviews. Every time another scandal breaks in the news, local and national talk show hosts call him for his perspective and insight. Not only is he not getting paid to be on these shows, much of the time he pays the long-distance costs to be on the phone with talk show hosts in all areas of the country.

Why Media Are Afraid of Larry Nichols

The first effort Larry made to get the truth to the people was to use the print media. National reporters had become aware of him during the presidential campaign. He became their best source of information for uncovering new stories. He bent over backwards to get them the information and the contacts they needed as they pursued each new skeleton in Clinton's closet. Those stories, along with his appearances on talk radio, were getting attention. Larry is the source who helped reporters break the stories that began it all. Before the election, he tipped them off to the womanizing. After the election, he gave them much more.

Jerry Seper and George Archibald of the *Washington Times* did a series of 28 articles between them that Larry claims were all a result of the information and sources he provided. Those national stories made the world aware of such things as the shredding of documents by the Rose Law firm, the break-in to Vince Foster's White House office the night of his death, and others. Nearly every major story that revealed another Clinton scandal came from Larry or a source that he provided.

The Clinton damage control team fought back by discrediting Larry in the eyes of the press to the extent that the use of his name in a story was perceived to damage the credibility of the story. The press, who owed their own notoriety as investigative reporters to Larry, dropped him like a hot potato. In spite of the fact that only a handful of reporters now call him for information, Larry continues to get information to the press through other people who help him. He has no concern over who gets credit for a story getting out. All he cares about is that the truth is told.

There are several reporters who have recognized Larry Nichols as a valuable, reliable source for accurate information. Chris Ruddy of the *Pittsburgh Tribune-Review* and Ambrose Evans-Pritchard of the *London Telegraph* have frequently relied on information provided by Larry, as have several others from time to time. They recognize the efforts made by Larry's enemies to try and discredit him, and have not let that stop them from using him as a source for their work.

Unlike the print media, talk radio hosts are not afraid of him. Both liberal and conservative hosts ask him for interviews constantly. During that first year of the Clinton presidency, Larry rapidly became the most sought-after talk show guest in the country, where he remains today.

Talk Show Hosts Love Him

Michael Reagan, one of the leading national talk show hosts, began interviewing Larry on a regular basis. Though Reagan is not known for bringing guests back to his show repeatedly, Larry has become a regular weekly feature with his reports on all aspects of the Clinton scandals and investigations. Local talk show hosts on Reagan's affiliate stations first learned of Larry by hearing those interviews, myself included. Local hosts would contact Larry after hearing him on Reagan's show, which brought him to listeners on a local level. Before long, he was a regular guest on hundreds of shows nationally and locally throughout the country.

It was during this period, early in the Clinton presidency, that Larry was the target of intense personal attacks from the Clinton damage control team. He knew and understood what it was all about, but had a tough time getting the press to see the tactics for what they were. Even his own family found it difficult to deal with the slings and arrows that were shot at him on a daily basis. Larry has the tough skin necessary for anyone who takes on a political foe, but his family did not. Nothing mattered more to him at that time than to regain respect from his father, who was suffering from terminal cancer. Larry knew that his father believed him, but it hurt him to know that his father disapproved of his pursuit of Clinton because of the price that had to be paid to do so.

A Magnet for Evidence and Witnesses

On July 20, 1993, Larry was watching a TV news program when he learned of the death of Vincent Foster. This one event and what was to follow helped him to easily show that he was telling the truth. He went to work and quickly learned from his sources inside the White House that Maggie Williams and Patsy Thomasson were at that very moment "ransacking" Foster's office, shredding documents, and hauling things away. Were it not for Larry, it is doubtful that the story would have gotten out to the press. His very existence provides a means to leak information to the press that would not get out otherwise.

Why is Larry so valuable? Because in the world of dog-eat-dog politics, there is no one else people can trust. Just ask yourself, if you had information detrimental to Clinton, who could you tell and know for certain that the person you were telling was not secretly loyal to him? People Larry has never met call him with information and send him evidence for that one reason alone. Everyone knows that Larry is not a Clinton supporter, that he never reveals a source who doesn't want to be revealed, and that he makes sure the information gets out.

About one week after Foster died, Larry received a very important piece of evidence. An envelope was left in his mail box. In it, he found a memo from the U.S. Secret Service, the people who protect the president of the United States. The memo revealed that Foster was found dead in his car in the Ft. Marcy Park area, near the George Washington Freeway. The memo also indicated that he died of a self-inflicted gunshot wound to the head. A copy of that memo can be found in the appendix.

With that information in hand, Larry felt very confident as he repeatedly told people that the reports of Foster being found dead in Ft. Marcy Park were not true. He didn't reveal that he had the memo right away to give others enough rope to hang themselves as they spun their damage control stories. He knew if he kept his mouth shut about the memo, there was a good chance he could use it later, knowing that the official investigators had a copy of the same memo. Remember, Larry knew how the Clinton damage control would handle this crisis. Though he does not claim to know why Foster died or what was being covered up by the Clinton staff, he does claim that the truth was not told about the death. He credits Chris Ruddy for the outstanding job he has done in pursuing the story, even while most other reporters ignore it and publicly criticize him for his efforts.

Money Offered, But Not Taken

Just a week before Foster died, some interesting documents were obtained from the White House as part of the string of investigations that continue today. Among them was David Watkins' calendar, on which he had written: *Pay Larry Nichols $116,000. Give it to his wife. Arrange a loan from Herbie Branscom.*

Larry says he was offered money to pay off his house. "They knew how much it was to pay off my house. They knew that I was about to lose it," he explained, saying they wanted him to "crawl into a hole and disappear." The offer would also mean Larry could get a job once again, stop looking over his shoulder everywhere he went, and save his family.

"I couldn't do it," he told me. "Heaven forgive me, I couldn't do it. I should have done it. I mean, I couldn't do it. I should have done it. I needed to do it. A smart man would have done it. A limited fool would have done it. If nothing else, just for my wife and my daughter, just to give them that. But I couldn't do it."

The Making of the Documentaries

It was a trying time when, in spite of all the challenges before him, Larry was not going to give up his quest to expose the Bill Clinton he knew to the world. He had been using the press and the talk radio circuit as fully as he knew how. The next logical step was to produce a documentary that could be distributed by video, since he knew the mainstream television shows would not touch it.

John Hillier, a video journalist, had called Larry regularly for over a year. Persistence finally paid off for Hillier when Larry told him he would now be willing to be interviewed for a documentary. Larry says Hillier told him that "he had done investigative video journalism and he had done work for Pat Robertson and Jerry Falwell." Although Hillier was unsuccessful at getting Robertson or Falwell to finance a documentary, he did bring Pat Matrisciana to Larry as someone who could help get a video made. Matrisciana had produced a few videos for the Christian market and told Larry, "that he would like to get my story on tape and he would use John to video it. It sounded okay to me. We discussed everything for a couple of weeks, then they came in to do it."

Larry told me he wanted to do the documentary as part of his continuing effort to warn the American people of his fears. "I was afraid that Clinton would take his circle of power to Washington. I was afraid he would turn the nation into Arkansas. That was what I was afraid of." Later, Larry says he came to realize that Clinton didn't have to bring his style of corruption to Washington, because it was already there.

Hillier and Matrisciana had been in Arkansas for a few days preparing for filming. Actual production would begin the next morning when suddenly Larry's world fell apart. "We were to commence filming the next morning," Larry explained. "I felt obligated to do something, but it seemed like there wasn't enough time, plus my dad was dying. You know, it was just a tough period, but I kept on. Finally, we set the plan that no matter what we would do it the next morning.

"Daddy had gotten progressively worse and worse, and we called my brother and sister in. It was just somewhat difficult to meet with Pat and John. That night, at 1:30 A.M. Daddy died in my arms. The last thing I told him was, 'Daddy, I'll get our name back.' Then he died."

In spite of what he had just been through, with hardly a moment of sleep, Larry kept his word and began filming at 7:30 A.M. on the documentary "Circle of Power." The process of filming was a difficult one. Everywhere they went, they were followed. It was also during that time that Larry was beat up and arrested on trumped up charges.

"We were moving around up and down the interstate, running from people. You just can't imagine. They were following us everywhere—*everywhere*. I got beaten to a pulp more than once during that time and got thrown in jail during that time. Hillier, bless his heart, he'd come barreling up with that camera. It was embarrassing. Whenever things would happen John would just ride in. He'd just stick that camera in somebody's face. You'd be amazed how people would back down when that camera was there.

"John used to say, 'You know how maggots are when you lift up an old log where they're in the dark. When the light hits them, they run.' That's what he'd say about his camera. Well, at one point it started to get to him and he started freaking out. He was somewhat paranoid anyway. And then, of course, being around me and seeing the things that were going on in real life makes someone who's not paranoid become paranoid. So you can imagine what it does to someone who is paranoid. Plus, he just absolutely positively was sure that they were going to get all of us."

During the production of both this first documentary and the next several months later, Larry went through approximately six different beatings. He says each was intended to make a point. Each time he led the cameras to a source of information, they would find him and beat him. Larry doesn't like to talk about it because he knows he can't prove who did it.

"It was always pretty well staged," he says. "Never in the face. It was always when I was by myself. That's why I don't talk about it a lot—because I can't prove it. They would always do it when I was out alone. I would go to the doctor but the problem is that he could claim I was in a car wreck. It was difficult. John Hillier, bless his heart, was wanting to video this stuff. He was wanting to go with it and blame Clinton. But I would say, 'John, you're a big time Christian. Can you swear this is Clinton? Did you see him order this? Can you prove it?' And he would, of course, realize there was nothing we could do. It's tough when your friend is being beaten to a pulp, but if we couldn't prove he ordered it to happen we couldn't say it, and still don't."

Under these adverse conditions, the documentaries were shot. The first consisted of interviews with Larry, Judge Jim

Johnson, and Larry's former attorney, Gary Johnson. Larry credits Hillier with getting the attorney on film, since he had gone into hiding after his nearly fatal beating. Even Larry didn't know where he was.

Credibility and Support

Tremendous credibility was given to the documentary because of the appearance of former Arkansas Senator, former candidate for governor, and retired Supreme Court Justice Jim Johnson. He had been a part of the political scene in Arkansas for decades and was well-respected by the public. Johnson says he was willing to speak in the documentaries because the truth needed to be told. He has also become one of Larry's biggest fans.

In the documentary, Johnson explained that "The boy [Larry Nichols] had to pay a high penalty in his credibility. He had to pay a high penalty in his acceptability [for speaking out about Clinton]. When the new evidence came out that supported everything that Larry Nichols had said, he finds himself, I think, probably, in the position of knowing that he had been exonerated." But just knowing for himself that the claims he made are true has never been enough for Larry, and Johnson knew that when he said, "He has not been exonerated in the minds of the people generally, in my view. And he finds himself, probably, in the position of wondering where he goes now to get his good name back."

As a result of getting to know Judge Johnson while making the documentaries, Larry and Johnson have struck up a rather close friendship. In fact, Larry considers him to be like a second father to him. Johnson has been the one person he has been able to go to when he's down and needs someone to give him a shot in the arm to keep him going.

"He didn't set out to be a defender of mine," explained Larry. "He had nothing to do with me." Judge Johnson admits that he, like the public in general, was believing all the negative press about Larry generated through the fabricated stories of the Clinton spin team. Each accusation was proven to be false, but the press failed to publish anything to clear Larry's name. Johnson, however, was astute enough to eventually realize that all the claims of Larry were coming true.

"He just all of a sudden figured out I was for real. Thank goodness he cared enough to get in touch with me," described Larry of the day Judge Johnson offered to help him. "Once he saw that I was telling the truth, he threw every once of energy and whatever else he had into the fray to help me. He just was adamant that we needed to get the word out. There was nothing gained. He didn't profit. It was him coming on and being the first person of any consequence who said, 'Take a look at this guy.' It was because of him that people even gave me a second look. Prior to Judge Johnson, I was 'the crazy man from Arkansas'."

At the time Hillier met with Larry to discuss the documentary, Larry did not know Johnson. When Hillier asked Larry for names of people who could be interviewed and had some credibility, he could not name any. Hillier found Johnson after reading a supportive editorial Johnson had written about Larry. It was a long shot, but Hillier was brave enough to ask, and Johnson was brave enough to agree to an interview for the documentary.

Larry was both thrilled and astonished. "The Judge is quite active, as many retired politicians are. He may be retired, but he's not dead. He is very well thought of and his opinions respected. They found him and they asked him, thinking of course that he wouldn't dare participate. I told them they wouldn't find anybody to speak good about me. I mean, it's not going to happen. But they found Judge Johnson, and he said without hesitation, 'Of course I'll help that man.'

"The Judge knows I have warts but he and his wife love me anyway. When I'm the bluest, when I'm totally outdone, when I'm totally defeated, he just has that ability to cheer me up and say, 'Get your britches back on. You've got a country to save. My God, you've got a country to save. You're doing the work of a hundred men.' He just has that ability to get my priorities back in gear. I just love him. He and Virginia, what can I say?"

The proceeds from the sale of this initial video documentary were used to finance a more in-depth report in a second production. The first was called "The Circle of Power" and the second was "The Clinton Chronicles." Public distribution of the first documentary helped give other people confidence to come forward with information and interviews for the second. For that reason also, Larry was very careful not to make a public issue of the beatings. His willingness to keep the beatings quiet helped prevent others from being scared away from giving information that was very sensitive.

Tremendous Impact Made

The first documentary served a tremendous purpose in that it provided motivation in a number of ways for others to come forward and add to the story for the second documentary. "The Clinton Chronicles" was produced within the next five to six months using the proceeds from the sale of the first video. During those few months, Larry would tell people he was not paid for doing the documentary, but says he could tell they did not believe him. He allowed them to believe what they wanted. The general belief that Larry "must be making a bundle" and the attraction of becoming a "talk show celebrity like Larry Nichols" motivated others to come forward with evidence. Still others were motivated when they saw the video, and Larry's courage to speak gave them courage.

"People would see the first video," he explained, "and they would say, 'I know something about that. I was this that and the other.' It wasn't like a design, it just happened. It gave people strength. Many a person that I talked to. I talked to a lot of people who said, 'I could never do this until I heard your story.' There were lots of people who came to me that I didn't take public. There were people who contacted me that Pat and John didn't know about, and I'm sure there were people who contacted them that I didn't know about."

So the first documentary facilitated the second both in terms of the necessary funds and as a motivating force to bring more witnesses and evidence forward that could be put on video. The additional witnesses helped to corroborate Larry's claims. Those who viewed the video considered his claim that Vince Foster didn't really die in Ft. Marcy Park to be rather bold, but what they didn't know was that he had the memo mentioned earlier.

Do It Again—Bigger and Better

The production was a similar effort to the first with more beatings for Larry, and intimidation for the crew as they were constantly followed. But they were able to complete the work, edit, and produce the video in time to get it out well before the midterm election. The well-documented claims in the video brought public discussion of the Clinton scandals to a peak, and Clinton's approval ratings to their lowest levels since. Every talk show host in America, from the smallest little station broadcasting to a handful of rural Americans to the largest nationally syndicated shows, talked about the accusations in "The Clinton Chronicles" every day for months preceding the election.

An interesting debate could be waged on the impact Larry has had on talk radio. The explosion of talk radio as a force to be reckoned with in America began just prior to the Clinton presidency and came on strong during his first term. Many will agree that the topic that drove talk shows was the many Clinton scandals. There was a fresh new scandal nearly every week to drive talk shows. Listeners tuned in more and more often to get the details that regular news casts had no time to give. What seems very obvious to me is that many of those scandals were made known through the efforts of Larry. Therefore, the question arises of which came first: "The Clinton Chronicles" or talk radio? The two items given the most credit for the landslide victory by conservatives in the 1994 midterm election were talk radio and "The Clinton Chronicles."

Falwell Checks Larry's Evidence

Evangelist Jerry Falwell called Larry after seeing the video. He said he wanted to send some lawyers to visit with Larry to see proof that the claims made in the video were true. Larry welcomed the opportunity.

"Well, in come his attorneys," described Larry of what he says was at best a trying time. "The attorneys didn't want to do it. They thought it was stupid on Falwell's part. They would investigate not only what was said on this tape, but they would make me prove any implied meaning. It's one thing to prove what I say, but going about it that way was a mammoth task that seemed to me to be overkill. But I sucked it up and took it. Finally, even though they didn't want to admit it, the attorneys had no choice. They tripled, quadrupled, and some cases more than that verified all the different points in the documentary."

Despite the preconceived disbelief of the attorneys, Larry was able to provide them with enough evidence that they had to admit the production was true, and that, if anything, it left out even more facts that had continued to become known. Falwell made an agreement with Pat Matrisciana to market "The Clinton Chronicles" on his television shows. Larry was not a recipient of any funds from those sales and has no idea how many were sold. But he is certain of one very important result of the Falwell effort: the requests for interviews on talk shows escalated even higher than ever.

Mysterious Death of John Hillier

It wasn't long after "The Clinton Chronicles" was completed that John Hillier went to a dentist. Larry said, "This is what we are told. Now this guy looked liked Charles Atlas. He was a health nut, strong, and exercised. He walks into a dentist office, sits down in the chair, and stops breathing. He was just in his early 50s. He was so phenomenally healthy. The dentist had not laid a finger on him. His wife was so scared she would not authorize an in-depth autopsy. They ended up saying that he had tiny air bubbles around his heart. I don't know. But once again, people do just die."

Accuracy is Number One

Since the first version of "The Clinton Chronicles" was produced, updated versions have been made as additional witnesses and evidence have come forward. Additional documentaries have been produced using footage from the interviews of Larry yet none of those productions have compensated him in any way. An industry of documentary videos on Clinton and government corruption has blossomed. As the additional productions have been made, Larry believes some of the work is questionable and less than professional from a journalistic view. Because of this, he always cautions viewers that he is not in any way connected with the decision-making that has gone into these productions. He says he will take responsibility for his own claims and remarks, but not for anything else that is claimed by others. Since the original documentaries were made, Larry has never been asked to give additional comments for any of the spin-off versions that have been produced. His original interview just continues to be duplicated over and over again. Because he knows some of the information in those newer productions is not accurate, he cautions viewers and is hesitant to work with the producers.

Larry is a stickler for the absolute truth. He does not want to even be associated with people who are less than truthful for fear it will be used to discredit him if he ever gets his chance to testify against the Clintons. He has proved every claim he has ever made to me and to everyone else who has requested proof. Talk show hosts like to go beyond the past and the present and often ask him to predict the future. Normally, he has only made such predictions when his knowledge of Clinton's method of operation and the facts at hand seem to provide a very predictable outcome. He is still kicking himself for a mistake he made early in the Clinton presidency, but he is not hesitant to admit his judgment was wrong.

"I had gone around all the talk shows and made a huge, bigger than gigantic mistake. I said on the talk shows that if they would hold hearings on Bill Clinton, that the powers that be around Clinton would never want their name out there. Politicians want all the publicity they can get, but the powerbrokers want to keep their names out of it. I said if they held hearings, within 90 days Clinton would resign under pressure from the power elite. Then here come the hearings. Gonzales from Texas was the chairman. It was an incredible total whitewash by the Democrats. Witnesses that they needed to talk to, they wouldn't talk to. So consequently they held hearings and nothing happened, and that was the day I realized we were in deeper trouble than I thought."

Regardless of Larry's missed cue, one thing is for certain. The awareness created by the two documentaries, coupled with the interviews on hundreds upon hundreds of talk shows kept the Clinton scandals as the focus of attention by the public, setting the stage for the most historic midterm election in U.S. history. There was no one more unprepared for the extent of the Republican landslide in 1994 than Larry Nichols. None of the polls indicated the type of defeat that the Democrats would suffer, and Larry actually went to bed early on election eve. He was awakened in the middle of the night by calls from the national press asking for his reaction. He was taken by complete surprise, as was Clinton.

Midterm Election Shocker

"Bill Clinton single-handedly destroyed his own party," described Nichols. "The people couldn't vote him out so they sent the strongest message they knew how, kicking anyone who even smelled like a liberal out of office. I know Clinton's facial expressions as well as anyone. Right after the election, if you looked at Clinton, he looked like a person that was in absolute shock. If there was a medical definition of absolute shock, Clinton was it. As white as a ghost. He was literally lost, just wandering. Everyone thought it was over for him. 'We got him on the ropes,' they would say. At the time I didn't realize Dick Morris was back helping him, but I recognized the tricks.

Saving a President

"All of a sudden, just in some subtle ways, more than just shock, I start seeing this rope-a-dope mannerism. If you go to radio programs back at the time, you will hear me on the air begging people to stop it. People were saying, 'He's toast. He's going to have to go. He's history.' Well, I started seeing rope-a-dope signs, plus I see Gingrich and Dole working with him. Here they had just gotten control of the house and senate, and they're working with Clinton to fast track NAFTA and GATT, which the conservatives were clearly opposed to. That was the moment, the play that turned Clinton around and saved his career."

It is not hard to identify loyalties when you "follow the money," says Larry. Don't forget who the powerbrokers are. Clinton was getting campaign support from the Stevens family, and Larry points out that so were Gingrich and Dole. In fact, Stephens' ex-wife Sue Anne, now married to Don Shula, was Dole's campaign manager in Arkansas in 1988. It was not unusual for one family member to support a Democrat and another to support a Republican.

Dick Morris, political strategist and talk show flop, was back working with Clinton after a rather hasty departure in

1988. It seems that Morris and Clinton parted company a few nights before the 1988 election after he fell victim to one of Clinton's violent temper tantrums. Larry says that Morris arrived late at night to give Clinton the bad news that the poll he had just taken showed Clinton behind in the race for governor. Clinton reportedly ran towards Morris and began to physically assault him, getting in some heavy punches.

Larry says, "Buddy Young pulled him off and Morris stormed out. Clinton said, 'You'll never work again,' and Morris said, 'I'll never work for another Democrat. I'll never work for Bill Clinton ever again.' That's when he left and started working with Republicans. That's what started it, when he got beat up. Believe it or not, this is a very significant tale because people don't understand how he worked for Republicans and Democrats." Apparently they kissed and made up by 1994.

Clinton was in deep muck after the 1994 election. He was no longer the "fair-haired boy" with the Washington power elite who had put him in office to begin with. According to Larry, they had been convinced by Stephens that Clinton was manageable and controllable, and yet in one election he destroyed many of their key players in the Democratic Party. Clinton was blamed by everyone for the destruction of what had taken so long to build. He was in the worst mess of his life and needed to find a solution fast. The Republicans gave it to him on a silver platter. They had won the big one and failed to capitalize and finish it off. Instead of becoming leaders, they returned to playing politics in the back rooms.

Just as he did in 1980 to win back the governorship he had thrown away, Clinton went with his hat in his hand to the powerbrokers and asked for one more chance. He promised to give them their fondest desires and they told him to push through NAFTA and GATT. Larry seemed to be the only one raising the alarm at the time. He tried to warn us, but we were all still heady with the success of the 1994 tidal wave.

"They gave Clinton one more chance, but he had to pull the NAFTA and GATT trick through. He was on a tight schedule, because once all those new, young turks got in there, it would die on the vine. So Clinton says, 'Don't worry, I'll get this through.' Then the power boys turn around to Dole and they say, 'You carry the ball.' And then Dole says, 'Hey, I'll get Gingrich.' And a pact was made that day. Then, all of a sudden you had Dole, Gingrich, and Clinton as a team, working against the will of the people together for the first time. It is so significant. And it was like I was the only one seeing it. A lot of people now say yeah, yeah, yeah. But then, everybody just thought that it was preposterous."

Talk USA Interview

I interviewed Larry on one of my talk shows and asked him to explain what happened back then. Here's the transcript from part of the show:

> *Bresnahan*: Larry, it's hard to believe the Republican leadership actually teamed up with Bill Clinton after the 1994 election, but that's exactly what you claim, right?

> *Nichols*: We were seeing the rope-a-dope. Had I known Dick Morris was in the mix, I would have been more scared, but I didn't know at the time. But that was the day of gloom. That was the day the deal was made. That's when we saw it. The coming together of Clinton and the Republicans and doing something together. NAFTA and GATT were the beginning of these two working together. Unfortunately, this is where it gets really crummy, Dave. I cannot prove Dole said to Clinton, "I'll take care of

the Republicans, you tend to the Democrats," but they teamed up and set a trap for
the new Republicans.

Bresnahan: Now wait a minute, Larry. What's
this trap you're talking about?

Nichols: The Republican leadership of Newt
Gingrich, Bob Dole, and Trent Lott as a
team. They literally set the trap for the new
Republicans, the young Republicans coming in who were planning to do the honorable thing and live up to their commitments
to the people who elected them. They had
walked into a trap that was set up for them.
It was a trap.

Bresnahan: Are you saying the Republican leadership set up the new freshmen "turks", as
you call them, to be taught from the beginning that they were not going to change
Washington the way they had promised?

Nichols: Their attitude was "We've got to get
these turks out of here who believe in something as stupid as a mandate to do what the
people want. They do not understand."

Bresnahan: Okay, assuming you're right and
the leadership planned to teach a group of
naive congressmen that they really weren't
on a mission to save the country, then why
did they help them get elected in the first
place?

Nichols: They helped them because, you see, until the election that's the way it would work. They helped them. That's what they had to do. But when they all won, it was a dynamic nobody planned on, and they had to learn to play a different game. Dave, you know yourself that the Republican party thought that these guys would give a good run for this seat or that one, but they weren't spending the happy victory money on them because they didn't think they had a chance. They were doing business as usual. Republicans played the game like they were trying to get people elected. Democrats played the game that they were trying to fend off the nasty Republicans. The unions make sure the Republican leadership and the Democrats get the most campaign money so the challengers don't stand a chance to win. It was all a big façade.

Bresnahan: So they played like they planned to win, but in reality, the Republicans never expected to win big in '94. You're saying it was a mistake.

Nichols: Wow, things went upside down. Here you were in just one day. Nobody planned on a contingency of what happens if the Republicans win. I mean, Republicans didn't plan on that. Nobody did. So now you've got Clinton over here in a state of shock, and equally you have Republicans over here in a state of shock, saying, "Hey, we know how to deal with losing, but hey, how do you deal with winning?" And then it just happened. Both sides came together on NAFTA and GATT. They developed a system. They developed a way to make things happen.

Bresnahan: The '94 election is when I was elected to the Utah House, so of course I was on a major high at the time. But it wasn't long before I was feeling like something was really wrong. I expected the Republicans to take Clinton on in a big way, but it seemed like the whole thing came to a grinding halt.

Nichols: Another little trick was going on. Most people were still believing that there were two parties, that the Republicans would be all over Clinton like white on rice. And here's this lone Larry boy out here saying something's not right. All I knew how to say at the time was, "This isn't right. Don't write Bill Clinton off. He's not out of the game." They'd say, "Larry, we smell blood and Clinton is toast."

Bresnahan: Dick Morris was quietly helping to bring the two sides together after the election and bring Clinton back from the dead. He made Clinton look like a Republican overnight and take credit for everything the Republicans did.

Nichols: Bill Clinton, pseudo Republican. The new Bill Clinton, with the help of Dick

Morris. He came out in an incredible piece of work. Bill Clinton took credit for all the work of the Republicans. He cut out the Republicans from having any position they could stand on. To the people, it looked like Bill Clinton was in charge and every deal was his deal. Think about where you would be mentally in this particular moment in time. This is the key to everything. Imagine me, I was screaming that something was going on behind closed doors. Nobody would listen. I didn't know it was Dick Morris at that time, and if I did, I would have been even more scared. After NAFTA and GATT, they stacked the investigations and had them rigged. Nothing would come of anything because they were all on the same side.

Bresnahan: Let's shift gears a little. You've known Bill Clinton for a long time. You know what he's really like and how he thinks. What is his political philosophy?

Nichols: His all time number one favorite politician, his hero, is Adolph Hitler.

Bresnahan: You actually heard him say this?

Nichols: Yeah. Now, he was not in favor of Hitler with the killing of the Jews. He admired his political tactics, his system. Well, the other thing that Bill Clinton believes, he believes there should be only a handful of rich people. That way it's much easier because you don't have many to kiss up to. There should be no middle class because that's what kills you. Everybody else ought to be paupers. Now when you achieve that, you have a smooth running machine. That's what Clinton wants. Just look at Arkansas. He wants the whole country to be like Arkansas.

Bresnahan: I wish you were joking, but I can tell you're not.

Nichols: People that are paupers are so busy trying to make ends meet that politics is the last thing on their mind. If you can keep them beat down, that is Clinton's utopia, what he thinks the world should be. Then you've got it made. That's no joke. That's what he believes. That's the way he lives. If you look, that's how he manages. If you look, if you take all the wrapping off, look what Clinton has done in Arkansas. There is virtually no middle class. Whatever middle class there is, it's controlled. It works for Stephens. It works for Tyson. It works for the state.

Bresnahan: Clinton's serious about this.

Nichols: You've just got to understand, Bill Clinton is no joke, folks. He fervently thinks that you must get rid of the so-called middle class, because if you don't, you have a bunch of people that you have to deal with. And he doesn't want to deal with them.

Bresnahan: Larry, you've painted a picture of a
very devious, deceitful, manipulating man
who will say or do anything to get what he
wants, regardless of whom he hurts along
the way. The public, polished image we get
through the media is a bit different. In fact
he is held up as a religious man. What about
religion? Is Bill Clinton a religious man?

Nichols: He claims to be a Christian, but, for
example, he has told some of the troopers
[his security guards] that nowhere in the
Bible does it say that oral sex is a sin. He has
looked, he has asked preachers, and no
where in the Bible, according to him, does
it say that oral sex is a sin. Religion for Bill
Clinton is a necessity politically, but beyond that I can't tell you, because even with
Bill Clinton I don't think I have a right to
tell you what he believes or doesn't believe.

And that seems to be the heart of the entire problem:
Clinton has learned to justify all of his actions and beliefs.
Larry says Clinton's popularity is high because the number of
people who will tolerate dishonesty and immorality outnum-
ber those who will not. This country was formed with a
constitution that was designed for a morally correct, traditional values-based society. America's values are ready to go
down the toilet and Bill Clinton is the one who wants to press
the handle to flush it.

6

Many Investigations— No Results

From the very beginning of the Clinton administration, there has been a continuous string of investigations into the accusations originated by Larry Nichols. No other person in history has been the initiating force behind so many investigations into the alleged wrongdoing of a president. Initially, the investigations gave hope to conservative Americans who believed the system would repair itself, because there were enough honest politicians left in Washington to restore the "republic for which we stand."

The charges made by Larry aroused people everywhere and resulted in a wave of new blood in Washington. With that wave came the expectation that justice was just around the corner, and restoration of honest government would follow. Tough-talking conservative Republicans were now in office and the people actually believed they would follow through with their many promises to get to the bottom of the Clinton scandals.

Much Expected After the '94 Election

For some time, it looked like there was an honest effort to uncover the truth. Committees and investigations were begun with accompanying promises of leaving no stone unturned in the quest to find the truth "no matter where it led." The conservative public began to stop clamoring for action because they believed reform was underway. They eased back on the pressure to "do something" and returned to more fundamental cares, like earning a living and raising a family. They trusted the freshmen they sent to Washington to perform an overhaul on government.

I can remember sitting in a hotel suite with Republican members of the Utah Legislature on Election Eve 1994. There was a great deal of rejoicing over the local and national victories of the Republicans that night, as would be expected. Within a few hours, a number of us were sitting around the room discussing the historic nature of the event and the impact it would have. A comment that came up over and over again was "The voters expect a lot of us, and we had better come through." Initially, for the public and for those of us who were elected that year, there was a belief that the election represented a revolution at the ballot box and there would now be a major repair of government.

It was an expectation that would gradually be dashed as investigations came and went with no results beyond business as usual. The young "turks," as Larry likes to call them, were learning that even though they had been recruited and trained by Newt Gingrich in conservative principles, it was Gingrich and the rest of the Republican leadership who were standing in the way of actually carrying out those conservative goals they had all campaigned for. The reality of Washington politics was to look like you were doing something when in reality you were just continuing business as usual. Say and do anything to get elected and stay elected, then after the election be loyal to leadership or be cut adrift. The Republican Party had control of both houses of Congress, but Republican leadership was in bed with the Democrats and the president. Regardless of platforms voted on at all party levels around the country, the leadership would pursue the goals of their special interest "true" constituents, but not do what was best for the people of the country.

What Made Them Cool Their Heels?

In very short order, Clinton was gaining popularity as he stopped the us-against-them partisan fighting typified by his healthcare battle during the first two years of his term. He took credit for everything the Republicans accomplished after the 1994 election, adding to the public perception that the "turks" they sent to Washington to bring about change had really done nothing. Clinton began to talk and act like a Republican. He had formed an alliance with the Republican leadership in the NAFTA and GATT coup. And, he had those files.

How quickly the press and the public forgot the issue of Filegate without demanding some accountability. Could it be that those files contained damaging information that Clinton could use to control Republicans who would threaten him? Isn't it interesting how one investigation after another started out with guns blazing, and, though millions were spent, in the end nothing at all happened? Larry has repeatedly pointed out the way Republicans have "rolled over and played dead" and the fact that Filegate was never pursued. "Clinton's got what he needs to keep one up on each of them," he said of the files.

Following the 1994 election, there was a reassuring message coming from Washington. Larry wanted to believe what we were all hearing, even though he was skeptical. "All you hear day after day is that they're in charge and they're going to have full and complete hearings this time. 'It's not going to be like it was with Gonzales,' they'd tell me. I heard on the news what they're going to investigate, and I knew they would need my evidence, but no one contacted me. They all knew what I had but they weren't calling, so I start having this sneaky suspicion."

It's important to realize that everyone in Congress had a copy of the Nichols documentaries. Numerous members of Congress or their aids had been in touch with Larry before and after the election. All the chairmen of the investigations and most committeemen had been in contact with him and knew what information he had available. Despite this, Larry was being ignored, along with all 40 boxes full of evidence. "It's like the girl who's all ready for the prom and nobody asks her to go," Larry says of the frustration of knowing all the work and sacrifice to document everything was being ignored. Then, finally, it appeared that someone was listening after all. A light was shining at the end of the tunnel, and the light was in the hand of Congressman Jim Leach. Unfortunately, the light burned out.

Hope Returns

"All of a sudden I get a call from some guy in Congressman Leach's office," said Larry of the day things seemed to turn around. "He says Leach knows all about me and wants me to know he will thoroughly investigate everything.

"He says, 'We know what you have said, but why don't you tell us?'

"So I tell him. He says to certain things along the way, 'That's incredible; it's a shame you can't prove it.'

"I said, 'What do you mean?'

"He said, 'Obviously no one could prove that.'

"I said, 'Is your fax machine on?' I faxed him the exact documents he needed that no one thought existed. "

"He said, 'Oh my God.'"

"We talked about something else. For example, I told him of the time there was a drug raid about to happen and the state had a warrant to arrest Barry Seal. They got a call from Col. Goodwin to stand down because he got a call from Clinton to call it off.

"He said, 'You can't prove that.'"

"I said, 'Is your fax machine on?'"

"When he saw what I sent, he said, 'They won't talk to us.'"

"I said, 'They may be members of the Arkansas State Police, but as long as you ask under oath, they will not lie.' In a matter of a few days they had testified.

"This went on day after day. We went item after item. He'd say, 'You can't prove that,' and I'd say, 'Is your fax machine on.' It got to be a joke. He'd ask for something and he'd say without waiting for me, 'Is your fax machine on?' This went on for six to eight weeks. Very intense.

"Finally, he calls and says, 'Great news. Everything you said was on the money. We had to clear up some things that others have said about you or attributed to you.' He said, 'It's exciting. You have not only proved what you were saying, but you were a treasure chest of information we did not know how to get.'

"I was starting to be suspect. I said, 'Okay, lay it on me. What's the deal?'

"He said a lot of nice things again, then said, 'I want our relationship to stay together, but you can't testify.'

"They said I had done the impossible, but I wouldn't be able to testify. I asked, 'What have I done?'

"And he said, 'You understand that you are just too hot. If we call you in, they will just have a field day with you being a Clinton hater.'

"I said, 'Wait a minute, I'm not. But if I were, what difference does it make if I have facts and I can prove what I say?'

"'Well, the congressman is afraid it would create too big of a spectacle and Clinton's people would be all over you, saying that you were too biased,' he came back.

"I said, 'Look, just leave me out of it then. At least when Larry Patterson and Roger Perry testify, it will make all the difference in the world.'

"He said, 'No, no they can't testify. They're too biased.'

"I said, 'Everybody who has something negative to say about the Clintons will be said to be too biased. You'll never have anybody who can testify.'

"He said, 'Well, I don't write the rules, I just have to live by them. Hey, the good news is that everything you said is true, and the congressman, I assure you, is going to bring all this out in his hearings. It will be explosive, and thanks to you, everything's going to come out.'

"I just said, 'Surely you don't think that. I think you're a good guy, but surely either you're one of them or you're awfully naive. You're no different than what's going on with D'Amato.' Then he fed me this stuff about Jim Leach being beyond reproach.

"I said, 'You can't believe all this.'

"He said, 'You'll see.'

As you know, not only did nothing come of that investigation, but they didn't even submit a written report when they ended. Millions of taxpayers' dollars and no report."

Kenneth Starr

About the time the Leach investigation was going nowhere, Larry was contacted by an attorney from Kenneth Starr's Special Prosecutor's office. He asked Larry to meet him at the I-40 truck stop in Morgan, Arkansas. He told Larry it was a "safe, neutral spot." Neither man trusted the other, so they played a few games to test the each other.

Larry described the meeting. "He told me they had troopers who have been around Clinton when he's done drugs. I said, 'No, you haven't.'

"He'd say, 'Oh yeah?'

"I said, 'I don't know who you're kidding, but you don't have any troopers who have been around Clinton doing dope.'

"He insisted, 'You have no idea who we've talked to and what we've talked about in the investigation.'

"I said, 'I know damn well. No one told you that because if they told you, they would have told me, and no one has said that.' And then he would say things of the sort you'd hear on the radio. He'd make those comments and I'd say, 'No, you didn't. That's not true.'

"And I would say things to see if he was for real. I would throw names out that were totally off base to see if he would bite to see if he was stroking me. After 45 minutes, he said, 'Okay, I'm convinced. Are you?' And I said, 'Yeah.'

"And from then on we started working together. He was trying to build a case against the McDougals and I said he couldn't build a case against them unless he got Governor Jim Guy Tucker. He didn't seem to think that would be wise. He didn't seem to want to pursue Tucker because of the political capital he would have to spend. I refused to give them evidence unless they did."

The attorney told Larry that Starr was quite aware of all his talk show appearances and had tapes of them. They hadn't come to him previously, supposedly because of the narrow scope of the special investigation. His example to Larry was that if Larry saw Clinton rob a bank, he couldn't bring it to Starr because it was outside Starr's jurisdiction. If Starr finds evidence outside his jurisdiction, there's nothing he can do with it except turn it over to someone who has jurisdiction. "And guess what? That guy is going to be a Clinton person," explained Larry. "You see how he's got it fixed? Half the people, or worse, that work for Starr are Clinton people—bad guys. They either report directly to the Clintons or worse."

Larry says that Clinton supporters in Starr's office are assigned to busy work. Important evidence is never discussed in the office and they do a security sweep to check for listening devices regularly. Getting a witness to talk with Starr's investigators is a challenge, according to Larry. If Clinton's people find out they will get word to Clinton and he will send "the henchmen in to shut them up, or really shut them up," it was explained.

Larry doesn't want me to reveal who he has worked with in Starr's office. He doesn't want it made public. I disagree but I have to respect his judgment. He explained, "Clinton knows exactly who I talk to in Starr's office. It's not a matter of keeping it a secret from them. It's different than that. A few talk show hosts know who I deal with, just like you, but we never mention it. We never mention who it is, who I deal with, even though Clinton and them know it. If Clinton's people ever find a legitimate way that I have repeatedly talked, other than just giving my statement, that I have repeatedly worked with my contact, or anyone for that matter, then they will brand us. They will make it look like Starr and them are a part of an effort by these 'right wing Clinton haters'."

One of the greatest ways Larry has been able to help the Starr investigation has been to obtain documentary evidence that has been unavailable to Starr through other means. Larry doesn't have to play by the rules. If he knows there is something Starr needs but can't get, he gets it. He won't say how he does it. Through confidential sources and other means, he has obtained extremely sensitive evidence located in offices Starr has no access to. If Clinton knew that evidence was being sought by Starr, it would disappear. Having someone like Larry Nichols available to get it quietly has been a tremendous asset to Starr.

Frustration and Distrust

Talk show listeners have become frustrated and impatient

with the Starr investigation because of the slow process. Many suspect Starr of being a Clinton supporter and believe he will never take any action against the president. Larry has explained the technical side of the process on the air in an effort to help listeners know how difficult it all is, and many have interpreted that to mean Larry is a supporter of Starr and believes Starr is legitimately going to take action against the Clintons. In reality, Larry has a very good understanding of how the system is rigged to Clinton's favor and has tried to explain that to people so their expectations will be more realistic. Larry will be as shocked as the biggest skeptic if Starr indicts the Clintons. But as he says, "Like it or not, Starr's our only shot at this, so we have to give it all we've got."

One of the main reasons for the length of time the Starr investigation has dragged on, according to Larry, is the process itself. If Starr's investigators want to talk to someone and question them, they can just do it. However, once an indictment is made, they can't do things so easily. Once that happens, they need to make a motion before the judge. Then the other side will make a motion that talking to the desired person is not relevant and not under the jurisdiction of the investigation. That kind of game would delay and impede things even more. So Starr will continue the investigation until all his ducks are in a row, because once an indictment is made, everything comes to a grinding halt. Testimony that takes days to get will now take months and years after an indictment is made.

When Larry explains these facts of life to talk show listeners, who are already frustrated with the lengthy process, they become even more frustrated and often take it out on him. "Everybody out there screaming for Starr to indict better watch out. Not only had they better have the case against the Clintons made, but they had also better have interviewed everyone they want to interview, because it is over the minute they indict. The Clintons know that. If you don't believe that the Clintons would not breathe, in one way, a giant sigh of relief, I've got property to sell you. Because right now the Clintons don't know who he's talking to; they don't know who I'm talking to. All of this is out there and they're very uncomfortable," he explained.

Larry says he still believes indictments against Hillary Clinton and Webster Hubbell are coming, if we'll all just be patient. The discovery of the trunk filled with documents in the abandoned car was "just a treasure chest of valuable evidence to prove Hillary, Bill, Hubbell, and so many others perjured themselves. Plus, it's the evidence that ties it all together. It's the missing link."

What is the National Press Waiting for?

What a botched group of inept people working for Clinton. They load the trunk with all the key incriminating evidence with a plan to dump it all. The borrowed, dilapidated car breaks down and the driver leaves it in a car repair shop's back lot. The owner can't be bothered to pay to fix it, so he leaves it there. The driver who borrowed it believes the owner has repaired the car and dumped the documents. The owner believes the documents are already gone and there's no need to deal with the car. And there it sits for about ten years until a tornado comes along and tosses it around.

How remarkable that the mechanic who finally popped the trunk and saw Clinton's name on everything was wise enough to call Starr's office and not someone tied to Clinton. All that evidence has already been submitted to the grand jury. Even more fascinating to me is the lack of interest by the majority of the national press in this remarkable incident. This should be the stuff all reporters would just love to sink their investigative teeth into. Most papers carried it as a minor "isn't this interesting" type of story, with the focus on one check. The average American has no idea that the trunk was absolutely packed with very incriminating documents, most of which have the potential to show that Webster Hubbell, Hillary Clinton, and other Rose Law firm associates have perjured themselves badly. Have the journalism schools in America failed to produce capable reporters, or is there something to the claim that Larry makes about a liberal press that refuses to go after their poster boy in the White House?

When I first began interviewing Larry for this book, he repeatedly mentioned that the Starr investigation had some important evidence, and, until that evidence was presented to the grand jury, he was very hesitant to talk about specifics as to why he believed so strongly that the investigation would lead to indictments, at least against Hillary.

Now that we know about the documents found in the car, once again it has been proven that Larry knows what he is doing and talking about. He is not some nut on talk radio, as some have categorized him. He is well-informed, knowledgeable, and factual. He is also very careful about what he reveals for fear he may impede the investigations. He has also done all he can to maintain his credibility as a witness should the day ever comes that he is called as one.

Not only has Larry accumulated the mountain of evidence he has submitted to every investigation committee, but he has also supplied witnesses to the grand jury. Witnesses who, as he says, have come out of the woodwork that Clinton doesn't know about. Because there are so many people who have testified secretly, he is not talking about them and the information they've given for fear that Clinton would figure out that they've talked. Larry doesn't want to do anything to jeopardize the process or the people. That's why when we first talked about writing this book, he made it very clear this could not be a book about the evidence. When I explained I wanted to write about the political strategies and dirty tricks used by Clinton, and not the evidence and womanizing, that is when he agreed to do this book. Others had come to him trying to get into his 40 boxes of evidence or they wanted to write all the sordid details of Clinton's womanizing. Larry was never interested in any of that. Larry has very consistently tried to find ways to inform the public of the way they are being deceived. He has never been sidetracked.

Are the Investigations Rigged?

Each of the investigations in the House and Senate has resulted in a familiar pattern. The real evidence, the significant evidence, the witnesses who can really shed some light on all of the corruption and illegal activities, are all suppressed. It's all for show. They allow the public to believe they are investigating thoroughly but they leave the most important parts out. Each of the committees has ended with nothing, and most of the time they don't even file a report. My purpose is not to go over each of the failures by each of the investigations, but instead it is to help you to see through the activities of one particular individual the kind of manipulation that has gone on and continues. His name is David Bossie. He and Larry have had a couple run-ins, and each time the event proved very revealing, not only about Bossie, but about the investigations and how they are manipulated.

David Bossie has maneuvered and manipulated his way around a number of political circles. He first made himself known in Senator Robert Dole's 1988 presidential campaign as his National Youth Director. By 1992 he had become the Executive Director of Floyd Brown's Presidential Victory Committee, which produced an ad and a toll-free number with recordings of Gennifer Flowers' alleged conversations with Clinton. His biggest claim to fame has been that he had a hand in the production of the famous Willie Horton commercial that helped to sink the Dukakis for President campaign. In 1994, Bossie became Director of Government Relations and Communications for the organization known as Citizens United, a conservative organization which sends Whitewater oriented tips, sound bites, documents, and story ideas to members of the press. He quickly developed a reputation among the press as someone who was a Whitewater evidence bounty hunter. He would lie, steal, cheat, harass, and intimidate to get information, documents, and evidence from people in Arkansas.

"Dave Bossie is nothing but a Clinton spy," says Larry, who offered some proof. On a number of occasions, Larry had worked with Ira Silverman, NBC senior news producer, on different stories. Silverman would come to Arkansas with a film crew, do a story about Larry and then NBC would kill the story and not air it. This time, Larry had told Silverman about Beverly Bassett Schaffer, Clinton appointee to head the Security and Exchange Commission. Larry gave Silverman evidence that indicated Schaffer had given preferential treatment to Clinton and Jim McDougal for a Whitewater loan.

"It was odd. Every time I met with Silverman, Bossie was there," explained Larry. Bossie had told him that he had made all the arrangements to get NBC to do the story because NBC didn't consider Larry to be credible. When he finally had a moment alone with Silverman, Silverman told Larry, "I don't know these guys. Every time I turn around, they're there. Don't you think they're with me or I'm with them?"

Silverman and his crew were trying to get to Schaffer for a comment and she was avoiding them. His crew finally caught up with her and Bossie showed up and "made a scene", wasting the investigation by Silverman, according to Larry. "We had been working for a year to get the go-ahead from NBC. They spent thousands of dollars, and we finally get a break and who pops out, but Bossie, to destroy the whole thing. There was so much controversy over getting caught that NBC wouldn't touch anything. Ira Silverman finally just quit." Either Larry is right and Bossie sabotaged the event or Bossie was extremely inept.

On January 15, 1992, the *Fayetteville Morning News* reported that Beverly Bassett Schaffer claimed to have been "ambushed" and then "stalked" all around Fayetteville by Bossie. The incident was also reported in the *Arkansas Democrat-Gazette* a few days later.

On yet another occasion Bossie and Floyd Brown offered to pay Larry for interviews and documents. They checked him into a hotel where they could meet undisturbed. They also brought another man with them who would later be caught stalking Larry after being paid by the Democratic National Committee.

At that meeting, Larry decided he did not want to be interviewed because they were just interested in doing a book about the women in Clinton's life. He didn't want any part of it. He went to the front desk to pay the phone charges for the room because he had made a couple calls. When he was handed the bill, he discovered other calls had been made from his room, all to Betsy Wright, a Clinton loyalist. Now he knew for sure whose side Bossie was on. All this was at a time when Larry was so broke he had pawned some furniture to get some spending money. He would have welcomed the money Bossie had offered, but he would not compromise his principles.

In a separate incident, Bossie and Floyd Brown were caught red-handed stealing documents from one of Larry's 40 boxes of evidence he had obtained. They were not caught by Larry but by Judge Jim Johnson. The judge retrieved the documents and sent them packing. "I very much know that Bossie isn't what he appears," says Larry.

Before long he got a call from Quinn Hilliar, Congressman Bob Livingston's senior aid. He wanted Larry to work with Bossie. Larry told him the stories about Bossie and voiced his concern about loyalties. Hilliar said Bossie was now working for Senator Al D'Amato and was a real "go-getter." He said to Larry, "I think you and Bossie have just gotten off on the wrong foot. I've met with him and he's just a good guy. Bossie's just kind of funny."

Surprisingly, Larry was willing to help. He explained, "I

don't trust him, I don't ever get near him, but here is Bob Livingston's senior aid. I don't have a lot of friends in Washington, so I try to be accommodating. I never give up. I keep telling him 'This guy's trash, and maybe you like him, but keep him away from me.' So Bossie calls me on a Thursday.

"He says, 'I'm coming into town. Get all your documents. I am D'Amato's lead researcher. Either get your stuff out now or forever shut up.'

"I said, 'Dave, come on in. I'd love to give you the documents.'

"He said, 'Good, I'll be there. Whatever you do, do not leave your home this weekend. Do not leave your home till I get there.' Which is kind of a weird way to say something. So I just figure he's lying and exaggerating again.

"I said, 'Bossie, everything I've got you'll have. Except for one thing.'

"He said, 'What's that?'

"I said, 'You subpoena my records. You get a subpoena. You request my evidence and I will give it to you. That way everybody's going to know that you asked for it and everybody's going to know that I gave it to you.'

'Oh, of course. Certainly,' he told me."

Bossie promised to fax the subpoena to him that afternoon. It never came. Larry wasn't as concerned about not getting the fax as he was about trying to figure out exactly what Bossie was up to. After all, he had told Larry not to leave his house all weekend. Larry called him throughout the weekend to ask for the subpoena. Each time there was an excuse and a promise to get it. Each time the promise was broken. Larry knew that Bossie was up to something, so he phoned Hilliar to let him know that his concerns about Bossie were justified. Hilliar wanted to call Bossie and ask what was going on, but Larry convinced him to let Bossie play it through to expose his hand.

On Sunday morning, Larry was watching the network

interview news shows when he learned that Helen Dickey (White House secretary who placed calls the night Vince Foster died) would testify before the committee the next day. Larry realized then what Bossie had done. He never wanted the documents—all he wanted to do was to keep Larry in Arkansas.

Investigators had previously come to Arkansas and interviewed State Troopers Larry Patterson and Roger Perry regarding their knowledge of the calls made by Helen Dickey on the night of Vince Foster's death. Several interviews took place to make sure their testimony remained consistent. It did, and clearly indicated that Dickey called Governor Jim Guy Tucker on the night of Foster's death. Instead of the governor, she got Trooper Perry, and told him that Foster blew his brains out in the White House parking lot.

The troopers and Larry were not being asked to testify to the committee, yet Dickey would testify that she never said those things. It was obvious to Larry that Bossie was making a crude, unprofessional attempt to prevent any of them from appearing in Washington and forcing the committee to hear their side of the story.

Larry watched on television as the committee made light of him while interviewing Dickey, and actually helped her to dispute the claims of the troopers, discrediting the troopers without giving them any opportunity to present their side of it. The committee actually referred to Patterson and Perry as "ex-troopers" and claimed that they "refused" to come and testify before the committee. They also referred to Larry as "some guy starting rumors and selling tapes."

Larry was furious. When he called Bossie, he was told, "Larry, calm down. We did the right thing. We know what we're doing."

"Is lying the right thing?" asked Nichols.

"No, you don't understand," Bossie replied. "I talked to Roger and Larry just this morning and they had changed their story. They changed their time. They're not sure of the time."

Bossie was proving not only that his was a Clinton spy, but that he was also inept and a terrible liar. Larry and Patterson had been talking with each other and comparing notes all through the episode, but to be certain, Larry called him on another line and told him what Bossie had said. Patterson confirmed that the accusation about changing his story was not true and that he had not been called by Bossie.

Ever since then, Larry has called Bossie a liar, and Patterson agreed with that assessment when I asked him. The two do not claim to know for whom he really works, but they say he cannot be trusted. The interesting part of all this is that Bossie continues to be placed in positions that are sensitive to investigations. Before D'Amato, it was Senator Lauch Faircloth whom he worked for. Larry has similar stories of manipulated witnesses and ignored evidence. Today Bossie is working for Congressman Dan Burton as part of his investigation. Burton continues to ask for evidence and witnesses from Larry.

Bossie Still at It

I wanted to know if Larry had figured out why D'Amato, supposedly opposed to Clinton, would take the approach he had taken. He told me, "It's just incredible. That's when I knew it was over. We had been had. Guess what? D'Amato was Bob Dole's campaign chairman for New York. Bob Dole is financed and controlled by Jack Stephens. Clinton is financed and controlled by the same Jack Stephens. D'Amato had a campaign coming up, and guess who he needs in his campaign to win? Stephens and the unions. Who is funding the advertisements for Clinton? The unions. We just got had, buddy. We just got had."

In all there are 16 different Congressman and Senators who have received evidence and testimony from witnesses supplied by Larry. Not one has yet issued a single report on their findings after spending millions of tax dollars. Most have suspended their investigations or, at best, are treading water. Because so many conservatives seem to think that Burton is the last great hope for truth and because Bossie is working for him, I asked Larry if he has had any form of discussion about Bossie with Burton.

"You bet I have. I've talked to Burton more than once. He calls me all the time and I keep warning him about Bossie. He tells me not to worry, that Bossie is just a staffer and not in charge of anything. Burton actually told me that I could send my witnesses to him and he'd interview them personally without Bossie present. As if that would do any good. He just doesn't get it. I asked him, 'If you had witnesses that nobody knows who they are yet, they're secret, would you bring them in? Yeah, maybe we don't come in and meet with Bossie, but how long would it take? I have people right now that are as fed up as can be who were ready to testify. We play mega top secret to get messages in and out. Clinton and they know I've got somebody. They just don't know who it is."

If Congressman Burton really wants to get to the bottom of it all, if he really wants to run a "fair, impartial, and thorough" investigation, if he doesn't want to place peoples' lives in danger, he will need to get rid of Bossie before Larry and his 40 boxes of evidence and numerous secret witnesses ever come forward. Without Larry, no investigation can be complete. Without the witnesses who have not yet testified to anyone, no investigation will survive the onslaught of the Clinton damage control machine.

If Not Burton, Who?

So if Dan Burton is not the one, who do we have that can provide any hope? Reluctantly, but hopefully, Larry says it is Kenneth Starr. There are many critics from among conservatives of the Starr investigation. Along the way Larry has had times of doubt and distrust, but in general has been a defender of Starr. Larry has been a significant source of evidence and witnesses, and he has managed to find evidence that Starr couldn't get himself without Larry's help. Does Starr know who the secret witnesses are? Larry says he does indeed.

Many believe such a witness or witnesses exist, but the identities are well-guarded. There are many things that Larry has confided with me that will not be revealed in this book or elsewhere. The identity of secret witnesses or even their area of testimony have not been made known to me. But from what Larry indicates, Clinton must be lying awake at night.

The fact that there have been many mysterious deaths involving people tied to the Clintons has been a subject for much discussion, particularly on talk radio because the mainstream media has missed another great opportunity for investigative journalism. It is not surprising to think that people would actually be in hiding in fear for their very lives. It is hard to believe that in the United States of America we have reached a point where people are afraid their own president would have them killed. Yet a good case in point is James McDougal.

Larry told me a fascinating story about what happened when McDougal decided to cooperate with Starr. The details would make a great television drama that everyone would think was fictional because the reality of what happened is so difficult to accept for the average American. The short version of the story is that McDougal had to be protected by Starr until he had finished giving his evidence. He was protected by the U.S. Independent Counsel from the President. The fact that McDougal was secreted away, moving from one part of the country to the next day after day with armed guards and secret hotel rooms never made the papers. He was at risk until his testimony was complete, although Larry says McDougal will be sleeping with one eye open the entire time he is in prison.

The only people McDougal could possibly give evidence to Starr about, within the jurisdiction of the special investigation, would be Bill and Hillary Clinton. Larry says he would be far more damaging to Hillary than to Bill. But, in actuality, Starr has no plans to ever have McDougal testify in a court of law. McDougal has no credibility as a witness because he is a convicted felon.

"Starr knew that McDougal would lie through his teeth to protect himself," Larry explained. "The only way they would work with him was for him to prove everything he said with solid documentation. I'm telling you, what they got from McDougal was volumes. It was huge."

Ironically, Larry says that McDougal was planning to sacrifice himself for Susan, his wife. "He would have done it. He really felt like Bill and Hillary had used Susan, manipulated her to sign some things. In the beginning he never negotiated one day for himself. He negotiated to get Susan off. Only when Susan and her attorneys attacked him and said he was lying, he said, 'Okay, cut me the best deal.' He never negotiated in his own behalf prior to them turning on him. He never asked for one day's reduction of sentence."

Where does this leave Susan McDougal, who at the time of this writing is still in prison on contempt charges? Will she turn? Will she finally talk? Will Starr cut a deal with her?

Larry made it clear, "You need to take Susan McDougal off your list for good. Number one, when Jim turned, Susan's got nothing. What's she going to give you? Even if she's got something new, she's a felon. She's got to back it up with documents like Jim did. She's got no documents. What's she going to do? All she's got is to keep herself in Clinton's camp. The only chance she has under the sun is to get a presidential pardon. Clinton hasn't pardoned her because he would be attacked immediately. He would be seen as giving someone a pardon to protect himself."

Pardon me

"He has got to give some pardons to avoid being led out

of the White House in handcuffs. But, there's a time that you can do things, and now isn't it. Some of this stuff could still have bearing, so we have to be careful. There are a half dozen pardons that Clinton will make. These key pardons shut Starr down."

Larry certainly brings out an important point. Clinton will not give pardons out of the goodness of his heart. Any pardon given will be strategically used to put him in a better position. Larry explained how he could pardon Hillary and bring an end to the entire Starr investigation.

"Hillary won't turn because she can't. It's either jail or a pardon. The thing that scares me is a negotiated plea of no contest where, if she pleads no contest, they'll hush it up and seal everything. Probably as part of her pleading no contest will be that if we're not careful Starr will sign a deal saying it will end there. More than Starr wants a victory, he's afraid of a defeat. I'm scared to death that if Clinton and them are smart with Hillary, they could give Starr a victory of sorts. He'll agree to drop everything if they let him look like he won a victory. There's no risk in it for Starr. I'm afraid he wants to drop it as badly as they want it dropped.

"That settlement, that negotiated plea, is totally unaccept-able to me. We can talk about it until the cows come home. When they plead no contest and drop it, then everybody's going to know that Clinton made a deal. Then who are you going to call? You can't call congress. You can't call the senate. Who are you going to call? It will be just like the Ron Brown thing."

In a nutshell, former Commerce Secretary Ron Brown was part of a special investigation and, according to sources within the investigation, was about to be indicted along with 54 prominent businessmen, including John Huang, Mochtar Riady, and James Riady. Ron Brown died in a controversial plane crash and within one hour, the Justice Department shut down the entire investigation. More than 100 investigators and support staff were herded out the door, all documents were shredded, and all computer hard drives removed. Ron Brown was no longer being investigated and 54 others were let off the hook. Larry is afraid that if Hillary Clinton is pardoned, the investigation will end and all others being considered for indictments will be let off the hook.

Will that really happen? "I don't know," responded Larry. "It's just one of many possibilities. If it does, or something like it, at least we can say we warned the people. Hopefully, enough Americans will be alerted to these types of dirty tricks so that they won't stand for it. Who knows?"

The damage control experts know how to sell their dirty tricks to the American public in a way that the majority will accept their explanations. In the case of Ron Brown, for example, they simply said, "Ron Brown is dead, so why continue investigating? Case closed." In the case of a pardon for Hillary Clinton, you can almost hear Bill with his announcement now. He'll say something like, "Those mean-spirited Republicans. Poor little Hillary, the mother of my child. It's below low. They came after her to get at me and I'm not going to stand for it." Larry says that's about the way he'll play it, and if he can time it just right, he'll do it when some other issue or crisis is in the news to keep the focus of attention away from a pardon. In addition, he'll have the liberal women of the world on his side defending him as a knight in shining armor saving his princess. Larry agrees and adds, "He'll say, 'I'm not going to let them do it. I'm going to remove the mother of my daughter from this vicious Republican attack on me. Those mean-spirited Republicans attacking this poor defenseless woman.' Then he pardons her and guess what? It shuts down the investigation. Starr is investigating Hillary. When she is indicted and Clinton gives her a pardon, then all witnesses pertinent to Hillary are let go. Just like Ron Brown."

Larry explained that the indictment of Hillary is out of the reach of Congress, which would have jurisdiction over Bill

Clinton. He explained that Starr will avoid Clinton because he does not want his success or failure to be in the hands of congress, which appears to be lined up to support the president. In fact, Larry claims that Republicans have gone out of their way to get Starr to back off. "If Starr goes through with an indictment against Hillary, that's a good indicator that he his acting independently of the Clinton people in Congress who have tried so hard to influence him," predicted Larry.

For Kenneth Starr, this is the ultimate challenge of his life. It makes sense that he might look for a solution that enables him to come out a winner, no matter what. To go to trial, regardless of evidence and witnesses, Starr takes a huge chance that he will lose. To indict the First Lady and then lose, would destroy him, and that is why a deal for a pardon of Hillary after a plea of no contest would solve Starr's problem nicely. He comes out as a winner without the challenge of a trial and the risk of a loss.

"It might be the right thing to do," comments Larry. "Because if you go to congress to prosecute the president, it just isn't going to happen. Bill Clinton is not like Richard Nixon. He won't do the honorable thing and resign. I know Bill. You're going to have to drive a stake through his heart to get him to leave that town, figuratively speaking. I'm telling you, Bill Clinton has no honor. The honorable thing is not even in the play book."

Starr's office no longer calls Larry. At one time he was on the phone and meeting with them on an almost daily basis for months. During that time, he became more closely aware of what they were doing and planning to do than anyone else on the outside of that office. He was a great source for news people because of his intimate knowledge of what was going on behind the scenes. Yet he never stepped over the line. Whenever he was on a talk show, he was very cautious and careful not to divulge information that could cause difficulty for the Starr investigation. There is much to this day that he has not revealed, however Starr no longer talks to him.

When the press was talking about Starr looking into reports that Webster Hubbell had been paid $500,000 to keep quiet, Larry commented on the Michael Reagan show and my show that in reality Starr was looking into evidence that showed the real figure was closer to $4 million. An attorney from Starr's office called Larry and blasted him. Since then they have not talked with Larry again, which does not bother him. What troubles him is the way the Vince Foster portion of the investigation was handled.

"He stabbed us in the back," Larry said of Starr. When Starr concluded his Foster investigation, he sent out a press release that said, "Based on investigation and review of evidence by experts and experienced investigators and prosecutors, this office concluded that Mr. Foster committed suicide by gun shot in Ft. Marcy Park, Virginia on July 20, 1996."

"I know that is not what he knows," said Larry of Starr. "He knows that's not true. Now, I'm not saying he knows Foster was murdered or that he even knows what actually happened, but he knows that he did not die in Ft. Marcy Park the way they said."

Larry doesn't know why Starr ignored evidence which contradicts what he put in his report. Such things as the memo from the Secret Service stating that Foster was found in his car, not in the park, as well as the Helen Dickey phone call to Trooper Roger Perry, and so many other pieces of evidence which at least point to the fact that Foster died somewhere other than in Ft. Marcy Park. What he does know is the attorney who had been given a full-time assignment to investigate Foster is now assigned full-time to investigate Wester Hubbell. Larry believes that perhaps because the Foster investigation was at a dead end, in that no explanation for his death, regardless of location, could be given, Starr may have decided to put his resources where they were most needed.

Starr needs Hubbell, and Larry says he almost has him.

"Hubbell has what is needed to get both Hillary and Bill, but it looks like he's been paid $4 million to keep quiet. Starr will have to overcome that," he explained.

The Chris Ruddy Factor

Larry believes that there are two developing issues, in addition to the many others, that have the potential to destroy Clinton. Even though Starr has closed the book on the Vince Foster death, Larry believes there are sources who have the missing information needed to reopen it and bring out the truth. He also sees the emerging story about the death of Commerce Secretary Ron Brown as being very destructive to Clinton. The possibility that Brown was assassinated rather than killed in an accidental plane crash has enormous implications.

Those two stories continue to be issues today only because of the work of investigative journalist, Chris Ruddy of the *Pittsburgh Tribune-Review*. Larry gives high-fives to Ruddy and his publisher, Richard Scaife, for their determination and courage to pursue the truth in spite of heavy criticism from their colleagues.

"I give more credit to Chris Ruddy than anyone else, including myself, for bringing forward the whole story about Vince Foster and keeping it out there. Chris has kept that story from going away, preventing the Clintons from just brushing it under the carpet. The Clintons will not be able to keep hidden whatever they have hidden on Vince Foster for much longer.

"Chris Ruddy not only does a thorough job in reporting, but he has a high standard for truth and fairness and a very professional manner. Because of that, he will continue to be a major force for Clinton to deal with. And thank goodness Scaife has the staying power to keep Chris writing for his paper."

Larry made it very clear that Foster and Brown are keys to unraveling the tangled web of corruption he says exists, not only in the White House, but throughout Washington, D.C. Because both of those stories lead to the names of the powerbrokers who control Clinton and other Washington political leaders in both parties, solving those cases would also mean exposing all the dirty laundry in the capitol.

7

Talk Radio

Larry Nichols started appearing on radio talk shows in 1991. He attracted attention because of his lawsuit against Governor Bill Clinton. Once the revelations about Clinton's womanizing were made known in the press, Larry began getting more and more requests for interviews. By 1992, he was becoming a regular guest on many shows on a daily basis.

Larry believes he is alive today because he has made himself such a very public figure. But he also believes that's why he has continued to receive periodic beatings and threats. "They'll beat me up," he says, "but they won't kill me, and it's all because of the talk shows."

The first talk show host of prominence to interview Larry was national talk show host, Michael Reagan. In his best-selling book *Making Waves*, Reagan says that Larry is "one of the most courageous, straight-up human beings I have ever known." He was willing to put Larry on his show when no other national host gave him the time of day. He says he was very skeptical of the claims being made by Larry. "I made him prove every word before we went on the air. In time, I found that some of the things that seemed so incredible at first were only the tip of the Arkansas iceberg," explains Reagan in his book, in which he devotes an entire chapter to Larry.

Many hundreds of local talk show hosts "discovered" Larry in the same way I did: by hearing him first on Reagan's show. Larry explained that after every appearance on the Reagan show, he receives 20–30 calls from Reagan's affiliate stations requesting interviews on their local programs. As the general manager and afternoon drivetime talk host of a Reagan affiliate station, I heard him several times before calling Reagan for his number. When I called Larry for an interview, I was, like Reagan, more than skeptical. But Larry was very pleasant and seemed genuinely pleased that I would call. In our preliminary discussion, he seemed very real, with no hype or exaggeration.

During that first interview, my questions focused on "The Clinton Chronicles" documentary video tape. One of my callers was extremely critical and quite harsh. Larry wasn't the least bit troubled and calmly explained how he knew what he knew. The caller then accused him of just making wild claims in order to sell video tapes. Larry countered by pointing out that he wasn't making a dime from the tape nor was he even giving out a number where it could be ordered. The caller wouldn't believe him. I called the producers of the video and they verified that they were not paying him.

Frankly, the talk show business is one in which hosts are deluged with requests for interviews by one person after another trying to sell tapes or books. It was hard for me to believe that Larry wasn't doing the same. After a few more interviews on the Reagan show, as well as on my own show,

I became convinced that he was extremely accurate and honest. I see him as a modern-day Paul Revere. His warning voice has been sounding out across the airwaves of America and will continue to sound out until he succeeds at exposing the Clintons as the criminals he believes they are.

Surprisingly, Larry will often give out his address and phone number when listeners ask how they can contact him. "Everybody always tells me I'm stupid for giving out my home number and address. Let me tell you, these people call me and they never impose on me. They never call me after eleven o'clock at night. Drunks don't call. They just are very kind, courteous people, and they check in to make sure I'm okay. They're just a pleasure to be around all of them," Larry explained, unconcerned about his safety by giving out his address. He told me, "If someone wants to get me, they'll find a way to do it."

Larry has not been paid for any commercial enterprise arising from all the videos, books and tapes about his quest to expose Bill Clinton. There are a number of people who have used his information and connections to produce a variety of items that have been sold to capitalize on his work, but they haven't shared the profits with him. Does he feel used? "Of course not. If it weren't for them, my message would not get out like it has," he says matter-of-factly.

Who do you know who would spend all day every day as a guest on one talk show after another without getting paid? When he's not on talk shows, he's playing detective, as he works his sources to uncover more evidence in the ever-widening story of corruption surrounding the Clintons and all who associate with them. I have come to learn that he is extremely serious about what he is doing. He has sacrificed absolutely everything, saying that there is nothing left to be done to him that hasn't already been done. No matter what, he will not relent.

His listeners help him out with small donations here and

there so he can pay the enormous phone bills that plague him every month. Some talk shows call him for interviews, but many stations make him call on his own nickel to be interviewed. Generous listeners send him a few dollars, which he uses to pay the phone bills. There's never anything left for him to spend on himself because the next $1,500–$3,000 phone bill is only a month away.

Track Record of Truth

There are many major national stories that were first exposed to the public by Larry on talk radio. Often when he makes his predictions, the skeptics laugh. But before very long, those skeptics must reconsider as his predictions come true. He breaks many stories on talk radio that reveal important evidence to the public. Some significant examples of proven stories released by Larry:

- The story of Clinton's womanizing and the use of public funds for that purpose;
- The indictment of Web Hubbell, along with former Arkansas Governor Jim Guy Tucker, and others;
- The shredding of documents at the Rose Law firm;
- The theft of evidence from Vince Foster's office in the White House;
- The Secret Service memo that stated Foster was found dead in his car;
- The Helen Dickey phone call stating that Foster died in his car at the White House;
- Details on how the ADFA was and is used to launder drug money;
- Details of how the ADFA issues loans that are never repaid;
- How chicken king Don Tyson has been under investigation for drug running;
- The story of Clinton giving a pardon to drug smuggler Dan Lasater;

- Details of drug running from Mena, Arkansas that continue to this day.

One major prediction yet to come true is Larry's belief that Hillary Clinton will be indicted. He has never said when that would be, but continues to claim it is inevitable. He says the mountain of evidence against her is enormous. He also believes she will receive a pardon, as will others in time. The fact that his other predictions have come true leads me to believe he will be right about this one as well. He's got a darn good track record.

There are actually many, many more examples I could give, but this list should at least provide a measurement of his reliability. As a journalist, I have found Larry to be indispensable because he knows what has happened and what will likely happen. He knows who can be relied on for accurate information and who cannot. Most importantly, he knows Clinton. Because he knows him so well, Larry can predict what he'll do in virtually any circumstance. Because of his many sources, he is not just a source for information on what happened in Arkansas while Clinton was governor. Larry is up to date on every major event surrounding Clinton because so many sources keep him informed on what is really going on.

Non-Stop Talking

Day after day, talk show after talk show, Larry keeps going and going. No sooner does he get through a week of 12–14 hours a day of interviews than a new scandal breaks and a fresh round of interviews begin. Does he ever get tired of saying the same thing on show after show?

"It's usually never the same," he says, "even when I talk about the same topic. You've got to understand that all over the country, I have some programs where the host has done a good job and the people are well-informed, so I can deal with advanced stuff. But then there are some programs that I do for the first or second time where the people are at the very beginning." Are all the callers and hosts friendly? Larry says absolutely not. "There are programs that I do where everybody who calls in hates me. I don't do just the friendly programs."

Larry has become a regular guest on 200–300 talk shows, getting called back once a month or more to each of them. Obviously, these are shows that accept what he has to say and want to hear more. In addition, he is asked regularly to appear on other shows as well. These are often radio stations in areas where he is not well known, and for that reason he likes to do them as often as he can. Sometimes the experience is good, but from time to time he is not treated well by the host or the listeners who call in.

A hostile host or caller is not enough to prevent Larry from accepting a return invitation, however. It will take at least three or four shows before he will give up trying to convince a talk show host that his information is correct. He has had many who, after several shows, say to him, "You've made a believer out of me." There are others who will never be convinced, and Larry does give up on them after giving them several chances. He's actually quite patient with some people who have been absolutely rude to him.

I asked him to describe how he handles the tough hosts. "Some people just break into fits and scream and call me names. I just say, 'Calm down. Calm down. Look, you're sitting here going nuts. Don't go nuts. We've got to deal with this and you asked me on, I didn't ask you.' You know, you just try to get them to calm down. Some of them get so mad they hang up on me while we're on the air. It's really funny. In a couple of cases where the hosts have hung up on me, the producer or the owner of the station calls me up and says, 'I'm sorry. That was totally unprofessional.' I don't do those shows again. With some people there's no point. Nothing I say will ever register with them."

Larry says the fact that he is not merchandising anything

enables him to accept interview requests on small stations as well as the large ones. People selling books and tapes often avoid such interviews. Larry enjoys them.

"I believe I am more effective," he says, "in going to places where they don't know who I am. I go to places where they don't know about Clinton. To me, that is where I need to be, rather than continually going to markets that know all of this. So I spend a goodly portion of my day dealing with every level of this stuff.

"I am resolved to the fact that I am going to have to wake America up one person at a time. I just mentally fathom that every day until I die, I'm going to tell people over and over until they hear and until they understand. And once I resolved that, then I don't have much problem with the few negative people I run into."

Larry is fascinating to watch as he talks to hosts and listeners. Believe it or not, he gets plenty of exercise throughout the day because he is on his feet, constantly pacing throughout his house with his portable phone. If his family is in the kitchen, he heads for the living room. If they are in the living room and kitchen, he may walk into his bedroom or even head for the garage. By staying on his feet, he manages to stay awake. There has actually been a time or two when he has fallen asleep in the middle of an interview, including one with me. He just starts early in the morning and keeps going until he drops. His usual day starts at 6 or 7 A.M. and lasts until 10 P.M. Larry gave me over 100 hours of interviews for this book, all done well after completing a full day of radio.

No Credibility, Say Mainstream Reporters

Newspaper reporters would seek out Larry for information on stories they were pursuing on a regular basis until he was challenged by Clinton and his supporters. Those individuals would make false claims about Larry, calling him an extremist, a Clinton basher. That label, right or wrong, brought criticism to journalists who quoted anything from Larry. Most of them stopped calling him. Once again, the Clinton damage control team controlled the media by making Larry "not credible" for use as a news source—not because anything he gave was ever proven to be false, but because he was given a label. Very few journalists today have the intestinal fortitude to stand up to their bosses and other critics.

I asked Larry how he gets along with newspaper journalists, and he responded, "They don't treat me well at all. Clinton and Stephens and them have done a very effective job with the print media. About 10–15 years ago, there were over 2,000 independently owned newspapers. Now that number is substantially less, as many papers are owned by the same people. Clinton and his people were very quick and very smart early in the game to make sure the media were on their side. If you look at what they did, they took control of TV and print media. So they had it sewn up. They did not take into account radio, because radio, to them, was music. They never dreamed that this talk radio stuff would catch on. I was able to come in under their radar before they knew it."

Larry says that Jack Stephens is rapidly buying up talk radio stations all over America. "Every month I lose maybe two to four stations. It's going to die off more than it has as yet. How many people are like me doing as much talk radio as I do?" Larry asked me rhetorically. "Does anybody hit as many talk shows as I do, day in and day out, and keep it up year after year? Nobody's doing it, and nobody lasts that long. I can see why. It makes you old."

No other guest I have ever interviewed is as precisely accurate as Larry Nichols. He is very concerned that unless he is truthful and accurate to the highest degree possible, Clinton will come after him. "I am capable of mispeaking just like you or anybody else. Hopefully, I would know better. If I say anything stupid, they're going to get it and Clinton will be all over it like white on rice."

A Life Saver

Larry credits national talk show host Michael Reagan for saving his life. "I was a dead man. It was when Mike sent that investigator friend of his down here. He spent a couple of months making sure I was for real, which I welcome from you or anybody. While checking me out, he caught a guy that was stalking me.

"It turns out [that the guy] was a psycho. We actually got him on video and on tape stalking me. We had him on tape threatening a state policeman, saying that he was going to kill him after he killed me. I mean, this guy was nuts."

According to Larry, apparently orders were given to the Arkansas law enforcement officials that this man was not to be arrested for any reason. Through the efforts of Reagan, talk show listeners and some congressmen began making calls to Arkansas officials, but they were in vain. Listeners were actually calling the Pulaski County Prosecutor's office, the Arkansas Governor's office, and finally Larry found out why no one could get anything done. This guy apparently had carte blanche to do anything he wanted and no one could do anything to stop him.

Finally, the stalker did one of those "dumb crook" deals news shows love to report when he "went to the state police headquarters to lodge a complaint. He saw Reagan's guy following him and thought the guy was from the state police. When he drove into the state police parking lot, he was drunker than Kooter Brown and was arrested on a DWI," Larry explained. He was protected by someone if he stuck to harassing Larry, but when made his dumb mistake, he apparently lost his protection.

"All kidding aside," says Larry, "Reagan saved my life."

Harassment as a Way of Life

Larry knows he is constantly under surveillance. "Sometimes it looks like a used car lot outside my home," he says.

Not only are they listening and watching, but they are a constant irritation, purposely trying to make life difficult for him and his family. "People from my past have been interviewed. Not only are they digging for something to use against me, but they appear to be trying to destroy my reputation."

He told me of an instance in which a restaurant owner was questioned. The owner was not only questioned, he was told what would happen if he continued to let Larry and his friends have meetings in his establishment. He called Larry and said, "I guess I don't have to tell you, but the bottom line is you can't meet here any more. You understand that I've got to be responsible. If my best friend comes in here drunk and rowdy, I've got to ask him to leave. You've got enemies and I don't need them after me."

Larry says these same enemies are purposely trying to destroy any credibility he has left in Conway. "They have scared away anyone they can who could even provide a support base. Anyone who could even say, 'Hey, we're with you.' It's a very methodical process. Once they've got everything eliminated that they can, then they hit. Then I'm literally somebody sitting out there on a limb. I know what their thinking is. Even people who believe in me right now, the recently-acquired moderate conservative, when they see that nobody in an entire community has anything good to say about me, they are going question whether they should believe me."

In another similar example, a professional in the area who Larry would visit as a friend called him and told him not to come by any more. He claimed that he was first warned by someone not to be near Larry because "he has enemies who are out to get him and they'll get you too." Larry's friend was even called by his own father, who gave him a similar warning to stay away. The father asked his son why he was hanging around Larry, and pointed out they could both lose their professional licenses.

Larry explained to me that there has been harassment within his own community. "People are going to friends, former friends, neighbors, former neighbors, classmates from high school, I mean, just an incredible operation. They're asking people if I ever talked to them or admitted to them about a law I might have broken, just trying to dig something up."

He has been harassed time and time again, saying that there have been "scary situations" since Clinton became president. "Now you see why I'm always upset. Not because of what they are going to do to me, I'm upset because I see people when I walk down the street hustling their children and hustling their wives out of the way. They walk across the street so they don't have to acknowledge you. It hurts your family. It tears my daughter up. This is the part that I hate to see happen, yet it happens time and time again." But then he was quick to add that he knows God will not give him more than he and his family can endure.

Secret Service Has "Keen" Interest

I actually witnessed what appeared to be an effort to arrest him recently. Larry had gone to California to speak to a group of talk show listeners and supporters. He makes such presentations several times a year. I attended so I would have time with him to work on the book, and was shocked to learn that the group who sponsored the event didn't even pay his airfare to get him there. All they did to help Larry was pass the hat at the event. I was in attendance at the presentation when local police arrested Richard Ball, a friend of Larry's who had come all the way from Virginia just to hear Larry speak.

The police took Larry's briefcase and told him he could send someone to pick it up at the police station later that night. When he finished speaking, Larry asked another friend to get the briefcase while he went to dinner with a group of supporters.

His friend arrived at the dinner and reported that the police would not give him the briefcase and that Larry was to call the police to make other arrangements. When Larry called (according to people standing by him as he made the call), his face turned pale and he had a troubled look when he hung up the phone. He explained that the person who answered the phone at the police station informed him that not only could he not pick up his briefcase after all, but that Ball was about to be booked and not let out of jail. Larry was told he was to personally come to the police station because "the Secret Service has a keen interest in this matter," which was what caused the look on his face and worried those standing nearby.

Larry hung up the phone and asked the people around him to go with him to the police station to retrieve Ball and his briefcase. It was interesting to see the look on peoples' faces when he asked for their help. Obviously the people realized the harassment stories Larry has mentioned on talk radio were very real and going with him would constitute possible personal risk. Consequently, there weren't very many offers of help. As it turned out, there were two wonderful ladies, one of whom had lived most of her life in that community. Because of her, and her late husband's, good reputation in the community, she offered the availability of their family attorney to help. Both women prayed openly for and with Larry, and drove him to the police station.

When they arrived in the station, Larry told the young officer at the desk who he was. The officer asked Larry to wait for the night sergeant who would be there in a moment. There was something about the way he made his comment that caused Larry to believe he was in a lot of trouble, and they prayed again.

Having been in similar situations before, Larry believed this might be an attempt to put him behind bars. To be behind bars in the Los Angeles area might mean he would not ever come out. It was at that moment that Larry asked the two women, loud enough for all to hear, for their help in the event he was arrested. They were to call George Putnam, one of the most popular Los Angeles talk show hosts immediately. They were to tell him that Larry had been arrested and ask Putnam to put it out on the air immediately. As it turned out, whether it was because the night sergeant heard Larry's instructions or whether it was due to the prayers they had all been saying aloud, the night sergeant arrived (empty-handed), abruptly turned around, returned to where he apparently came from, and came back with the briefcase.

Not to withhold the details of the arrest of Richard Ball, but until it is resolved legally, suffice it to say the night sergeant told Larry and his friends that the arrest of Ball and the taking of the briefcase were all a mistake. He presented Larry with the briefcase, and told the three of them that Ball would be released with no problem after he had completed the booking process. He also told them that the item which caused the incident was "almost hot." One of the women asked, "Is that like being almost pregnant?" The question was ignored.

There have been many events which could be considered mysterious, if not dubious that Larry has reported to me and frequently spoken of on talk radio. The frightening reality of what he goes through on a regular basis was made clear to me and approximately 600 others who were in attendance at the speaking engagement where this all took place. It was astonishing to me, not only that there has been a continuous series of what could be considered harassment incidents, but how easily a contrived foul up could land Larry—or anyone—in jail.

It appeared that there was some relationship between what happened at this event and a group of protesters who were causing a disturbance at the door to the facility where he was speaking that night. The protesters created enough of a disturbance that someone called the local police. Those protesters claimed to represent Lyndon LaRouche's organization. Apparently someone made comments to the police about evidence in Larry's briefcase. Perhaps they believed that making those claims would result in his arrest. However, when the police arrived, it was Ball who was holding the briefcase. If Larry had been holding the briefcase, the outcome might have been very different.

It appears that when the police ran a background check on Larry, they ran into some type of computer notice to contact the Secret Service. When the police arrived to make the arrest, they wanted Larry, not Ball.

Remember the story mentioned in Chapter 6 about the warning Larry received? He was told an attempt would be made to arrest him on a weekend, that he wouldn't live until Monday. Could it be that some type of notice in the computer records would facilitate that happening? Is Larry in danger anytime a law enforcement officer looks up his record?

When they were all reunited, Ball revealed that he was about to be transported to the Los Angeles County Jail when he was suddenly released. If Larry had been arrested instead of Ball, he would have ended up at the county jail and may not have survived the weekend. There are plenty of stories of things happening in that jail. The least little thing can have harmful, if not fatal, complications in his life. That is one of the reasons has asked me to be so very careful about what is said, and how it is said, in this book.

This is just a recent example of the challenges Larry faces every day. But this doesn't discourage him in any way. In fact, he becomes even more motivated to work harder to inform people about what is going on. Each day he just picks up the phone and keeps talking about what he claims to be the most corrupt president this country has ever had.

He believes talk radio is the best way to get his message to the people of grassroots America, and he believes he must maintain his presence on talk radio to stay alive. "There are ten gazillion people in this nation who have never heard of me, don't know who I am. I need to keep going until they all get to hear my story. When enough people know Clinton's tricks and how he fools them all, then maybe they'll say, 'Oh, now we see what that guy's been doing.' That's the only way to stop Clinton and those who will follow after him."

8

Nicholisms

The strategy of Larry Nichols in his quest to expose what he says are the crimes of Bill and Hillary Clinton is one which is unique, well-designed, and comes as a result of his knowledge of the damage control tactics of the Clinton spin team. The rules that govern everything he does are what he likes to call his "Nicholisms."

Make It Cool to Be Honest

Larry tells radio audiences, "You know, we've got to make it cool to be honest. We've got to make it cool to be good again. Right now Clinton is saying to your children, 'If you lie cheat and steal really well, you can get to be president too.' He's telling your kids, 'There are things that you won't do because your old mommies and daddies told you it wasn't good, so you don't do it. Children of America, it's because you don't have this total willingness to do what it takes that you'll never be president.' Is that what you want your kids to be taught? Is that the lesson you're teaching your kids? That's the less Bill Clinton's teaching them."

It is interesting to note that cadets at our nation's military academies have an honor code that says, "We will not lie, steal, or cheat nor tolerate among us anyone who does." Shouldn't that honor code apply to the politicians who select the cadets who go to the academies? Shouldn't that honor code apply to all of the military, even after they graduate from the academies? Shouldn't that honor code apply to the commander-in-chief of those cadets?

Larry says the heart of the problem is the demise of the two-parent family and traditional moral values. He says that corruption in government is now widespread and accepted by the public to the extent that they believe the two go hand-in-hand. At one time, if a politician was caught with his hand in the cookie jar, he was forced to resign or worse. Now, when a politician is exposed for corrupt practices, the public reacts with a "So what?" attitude because they expect their politicians to be corrupt. Over the years, the public has been led to believe that corrupt practices are a necessary part of getting the job done. People believe that in order for their elected leaders to protect their entitlements, protect their jobs, protect the government workers, protect the union workers, build the roads, build the schools, and keep it all afloat that they have to be corrupt or those things won't happen. The public seems to believe it is a necessary price to pay.

Larry has a strong faith in God and is discouraged with organized religion in America. He believes many of the religious leaders in the country have let their congregations down when it comes to warning the people about corruption in government.

"I believe very strongly in God," he says. "I walk closer

with him now than ever in my life. But, unfortunately, I've learned that many churches are not houses of the Lord anymore. If the churches are really what they say they are, then even the dumbest priest or preacher can see the evil around Clinton. Why aren't they talking about it?"

He is frustrated that the churches, where strong moral values and Christian principles are supposed to be taught, have not been pointing to the evil which is so obvious to him. He says he believes this is because the government could take away the non-profit status of a church for speaking out on political candidates and office holders.

He gave an interesting explanation for the state of the nation when he said, "Today the Devil could be president and 60 percent of the people would say that's okay. You better mix politics and religion because something's wrong. So when you ask me if I believe in the Lord, I do. As much as you, no more than you, but as much as the best. Do I live by His word every day? No. Do I read the Bible every day? No. Can I quote you scripture? No. Can I pick up the Bible and read it and learn it? Yes. Will I do it? No.

"I don't understand why God put me in this place. You'd think he'd pick somebody that's good. You'd at least think he'd pick someone that goes to church every Sunday. You'd at least think he'd at least pick a deacon; maybe not a preacher, but a deacon at least. But he didn't. I firmly believe that whatever my mission is, that when I go and meet St. Peter, I can say, 'St. Peter, I've done good this time.' I've asked forgiveness and the Lord has forgiven me. The problem is, I can't forgive me and I can't forget—not yet. The best thing I can do right now is to do the best that I can.

"There are some really great Christian people out there. Well, I'm not one of them. I try, but seem to fail quite regularly. But you see, we had to have somebody. Somebody who will fight these people in the dirt where they live. Because if we won't get in the dirt and claw and scratch with these people, how are we going to win?

"You know what Clinton and them count on? They count on you being good. They count on you. You cannot fathom doing the same things they are willing to do. You can't do it. They count on it. In my world, there are times when you should tell the truth and there are times when you had better shut up. Now there used to be a time when lying would be just fine for me. But at least I'm over that. There are times when you've got to do what you've got to do."

The problem Larry has willingly faced as he has valiantly tried to expose evidence about the Clintons is that in order to expose them, he has had to be willing to give up everything he has and be willing to endure physical beatings as well as beatings in the press. He has been turned in to a sideshow, and that has scared away the investigators, mainstream press, and people of Conway. It has not scared away Larry Nichols.

When it all began, he was alone in his effort and didn't have a talk radio audience like he does now. In the beginning, it took a great deal of courage to be willing to do what he did by confronting Clinton. Remarkably, it was back then that Larry developed a game plan that he knew would take a long time to pursue, but he believed that if he never gave up he would one day succeed.

Use the Other Man's Force on Him

"You learn in martial arts," Larry told me, "that in all things it's best to use the other man's force on him rather than trying to out do his strength. If you try to beat your opponent by being stronger than him, well, you just can't do it. This is an important key to defeating any attacker. You must use the other man's force on him."

In the beginning, Larry concluded that he must not let the Clinton damage control team succeed in breaking him. He knew he must be willing to give up everything, and, after that sacrifice, he must be still standing ready to fight some more.

Larry explained, "When you've been attacked by the Clinton spin machine, and everybody knows that helping you exposes them to the wrath of this machine, nobody comes near you. By design it's intended to kill your soul. That's when people have nervous breakdowns, that's when people lose their families. That's when people kill themselves."

Larry says the goal of the attacks on him was to destroy his family as well. By making his family suffer, Larry was expected to give in to the pressure to back off. What was the impact on his family? He explained, "You tell your wife and daughter, 'I lost my job, but I'll get another job and it's going to be okay.' Of course, then you don't get another job and you tell them, 'Look, I lost the job, but we'll keep our house.' Then you don't. Then you tell them, 'Well, we lost the house but we'll keep the cars.' Then you don't. Then you tell them, 'Well, we lost the cars but we'll keep the TV,' and it goes. What happens is that your family dies every step of the way with you. You see, you can't do something about it, but they can. They can leave. That's what snaps most people."

But Larry is not "most people" nor is his family. There is no question that Kerry and Beth Nichols are exceptional people who deserve a great deal of credit and recognition for what Larry has been able to do and for what they have endured. The situation certainly has been far from being a rosy one, but his enemies must have expected his family to leave him long ago.

He knew that for others in his position, the way out was to disappear. "There's only one way out. Take your licks and leave. Get away and never stick your head up again. You have to become something else. Never stick you head up again. If you're a banker, never be a banker again, because somebody's going to check, and when they do, it starts the cycle all over again.

"If you're good enough to get to the top of your field, when you go off and start all over again, you'll get to the top of your new field again. The problem is when you do, they're going to lay in wait and take your head off when you stick it up. That's how they forever keep you down. Eventually they break you and you have an nervous breakdown, or you kill yourself. The only way out is break and run. Never stick your head up. Never succeed. I mean *never*. Go get a job digging ditches and you stay there. Just be glad to be out of it with your skin and your family."

Larry wouldn't and didn't do that. He knew that if he could "use the other man's force on him", he stood a chance of winning. Police officers are able to stay active as they get older because they are trained to use the other man's force against him and thereby defeat attackers who are younger, bigger, and stronger. Larry said, "Strength doesn't mean anything. Just get the other guy going in a direction he's headed on his own and use that against him."

Why haven't the usual tricks worked to stop Larry?

Expose Them First

Larry says, "I know the drill." Indeed he does. Since he was once part of Clinton's damage control team, he knows what Clinton would do in virtually any situation. And, by properly anticipating what will happen, he can expose that damage control trick before it is even made. Every time Clinton is attacked, he will, in some form, deny the claim, destroy the person making the claim, and delay any action about the claim for as long as possible. Knowing this enables Larry to easily tell people what to expect before it happens.

This one Nicholism goes to the heart of the entire purpose of this book. Larry believes that the more people who know the damage control tactics in use by Clinton and other politicians, the easier it will be for him to warn people when those tricks are being use. Getting the word out so people will be knowledgeable brings up the next Nicholism.

Dig In Your Heels Until They Understand

From the beginning, Larry has taken advantage of every form of communication to try to teach people what he has discovered about the Clintons. Obviously, he has made excellent use of talk radio, talking to hosts on hundreds of stations in all areas of the country. In addition, he has jumped at every chance for media interviews, documentaries, or speaking engagements. Amazingly, he gives out his home phone all the time and gladly spends whatever time is needed on the phone to educate people one at a time. He considers this book as just one more vehicle to help people understand what is happening. He also knows that if people know what the damage control tactics are, when he tells them what will happen before Clinton actually does it, people will see that Larry has given them accurate information and they will not be deceived by the tactics.

Always Stay the Course

Anyone else would have been discouraged and quit, but the shenanigans that brought an end to the suit Larry filed against Clinton just pushed Larry into another round of the battle. He won some ground and knew he could gain more, a little at a time. He knew that his enemies had not counted on the fact that he has another rule he follows: "Always stay the course no matter what they do to you."

"I've proven that I'm willing to do what it takes and not give up. Sure, I'm stupid. I don't worry about little things like pain. I will do what I came to do and I will expose the Clintons and I will see them indicted. Starr may do it. I'm not sure. I hope so. But if not then I'll find another way. You have to keep going no matter what."

Time Has No Meaning

Larry never lets himself become pressured by someone's deadline. To explain how this is important to his efforts, he said, "If you say you are going to walk from Utah to Arkansas and will do whatever you have to do, you'll get there. To succeed in such a challenge you cannot plan what day you will arrive. It won't be easy, but you'll do it. Most Americans want what they want when they want it. That's where they go wrong—they establish a time frame." Larry has been very successful and has spent the past eight years without giving up, partially because "time has no meaning."

Everything we do in our society is set to a specific goal of completing a task by a certain time. We work a 40-hour week, we may have to meet a quota, and everything comes with a time it starts and stops. In fact, there are time management seminars and positive mental attitude types of training the reinforce the need to accomplish a goal by a specific time. Larry says all that does is place added stress and help ensure failure, because most people do not complete their goals by the time they plan.

The application of "time has no meaning" as a principle rule of operation is very significant to Larry. He does not let anyone place a deadline on anything he does. This book is a good example. When we first began our interviews, I told him I wanted to get it done in six to eight weeks. He didn't say anything. By the time six to eight weeks had come and gone, I had learned the "time has no meaning" principle and have not pushed for a completion date again. Getting it done—and getting it done right—has been the goal. There has been no goal to complete it by a certain date.

The media have become frustrated by this principle when they try to get Larry to do something by a deadline. Larry says he will not play their game when they tell him, "Provide us the information we want and do it our way to meet our deadline or we'll call you a liar in the story."

He says, "No matter what they do, no matter what they say, I refuse to let them get me down. I refuse to let them cause me to fail. The way they do that is to put on me some time limit that I have to produce something by, which puts me on a schedule that I can't keep to meet their deadline. They lose a story and a source. I lose everything. So time has no meaning."

There is one more very important part of Larry's strategy. It is so important that I have concluded that it would not be wise for his enemies to know what it is. Suffice it to say that as long as he adheres to the other principles, this one will eventually bring him victory. The only problem for all of us is that we live in a world where time is everything, and Larry functions in a world where time has no meaning. As a result, we become impatient while we watch and wait for the success Larry is seeking.

Convince the Undecided

Those who call Larry a Clinton hater are short-sighted. They need to look at the fact that he criticizes the Republican leadership as much, if not more, than he criticizes Clinton. The claims he makes cannot be called partisan nor un-founded. Yet he knows he cannot change many minds, so he doesn't try. He spends his time and effort at keeping his base of support strong and winning new supporters from among the undecided. He believes that approximately 20 percent of Americans are undecided on the issues concerning Bill Clinton. He gave an interesting description of how America is divided up among Clinton lovers, Clinton haters, and the undecided.

Right now we are at the most dangerous moment in the history of our nation, according to Larry. He believes the danger lies in the fact that the American people are so easily deceived, and that even when they see evidence of corruption, they ignore it. Such a condition makes the country ripe for the master of deception. Larry says, "Right now, Clinton could pull off his mask and reveal that he's really Satan and say to the people, 'I'm really your president. By the way, check your checkbooks, folks. Because as long as I'm in charge, you're still going to have your government job, you're still going to get your welfare check, you're still going to get to be what you want to be, and, by the way, I'm going to put a hundred thousand policemen on the street (even though I haven't yet). I do all this because I feel your pain.

"'Now don't you all be afraid that I'm really Satan, because you've already seen that as long as I'm here you get what you want as we head over the bridge to the 21st century. Do you want to go over that bridge with the mean old Republicans, who will make you hurt and take these nice things away, or do you want to go with me?'

"'Hey, everybody has a little devil in them. Some people think this nation is going to go to hell. Nations can't go to hell. People can go to hell. I know some of you still believe in God. God wants you to hurt. Do you want to hurt? I don't want you to hurt. So, if you're still basically good and you believe in God, then one day you can all repent and go to heaven in the end. Eat, drink, and be merry, for tomorrow we die and go to heaven. Besides, I'm just like you. You've got a little devil in you too, so you need to forgive me and overlook everything because I'm really doing so many good things for you.'

"Do you realize 60 percent of the people in this nation would buy that routine?" asked Larry. "Now do you see why I fight? This is why I do everything I do, because we must stop this now if we are going to return this country to it's moral roots." He believes that about 40 percent of Americans love Clinton and will support him regardless of anything. He says another 40 percent are convinced Clinton is evil and corrupt, and the remaining 20 percent are the swing voters who just don't care one way or the other. Those are the people he's trying to reach.

Everything Begins With One

You cannot put both shoes on at once. You have to start with one. Larry takes the same approach to building his base of support among the American people. He knows that this is a slow, steady process and he is willing to literally do it one person at a time. That's why he gives out his home phone number on the air. When people call, he takes the time to answer their questions and spend whatever time is needed to help them understand.

One of Larry's biggest concerns about the American public is that they will wait for a super hero to save the day or wait for the cavalry to ride in. He doesn't like being called a hero, because he's afraid the people will sit back and wait for him to slay the Clinton dragon by himself. So Larry is building his own cavalry, one person at a time.

Anything is Fair

Larry explains, "If you are going to battle an absolute liar, you must be willing to go after him on his level. This is the hardest part for all good, conservative, Christian Americans to understand. You have to play the game at his level or you get beat. Remember, he is counting on you to be good. I've used dirty tricks to get what we need. When I am dealing with him, anything is fair.

"When I am dealing with you and the people in radio land, I have got to absolutely tell the truth. And the bad news about absolute truth is that sometimes you have to tell the truth about stuff you don't want to tell the truth about."

In other words, when dealing with an enemies who will lie, steal, cheat, and use deception to accomplish his goals, Larry says he must be willing to confront them on their own level. The same tactics must be used on the enemies that they use on others. Larry calls this "getting down in the mud". He says that otherwise, they will eat us alive.

Don't Try to Save the World

Evil is everywhere. Corruption is everywhere. According to Larry, Clinton and his damage control squad are the best, but they are not alone. The problem is widespread at all levels of government. It took a long time to get that way and will take a long time to change.

Larry says he has the ability to stop Bill Clinton but that "saving the world isn't on my list." Not that other Bill Clintons of the world could not also be stopped, but he believes one at a time is all he can hope to achieve.

"I'm not stupid," said Larry. "I know that if we can expose Clinton enough, he can be brought to justice. Maybe not in actual court, but in the eyes of the people. Getting him to court is out of my hands, so I just expose the facts. If people are smart, they will look at what I'm doing and realize that they can do it as well at their local and state levels. Hopefully, enough people will start cleaning up enough so we will never have another Clinton. We must each find that one cleanup job that needs to be done, focus on that and eventually it can be done. When we try to save the whole world at once we will never make it.

"It all begins with one, and time has no meaning. Those principles will enable us to find our own individual victories and each victory added together just might restore honor and greatness to our country again," said Larry hopefully.

"So What?"

Clinton keeps America in a state of "So what?" by sticking to his proven damage control strategies. He knows exactly what to do with each new scandal to properly deny, destroy, and delay. Each time he furthers the attitude of "So what?" in the minds of the American people. Until that progressive apathy changes, he says Clinton will win and he will lose.

"As long as Clinton keeps following the damage control rules that let him get caught taking money from the Communist Chinese and giving them preferential treatment, he is violating the national security of this nation. Nothing will change until the people realize the danger we are in," Larry explained. "Boy that's big, but here's the drill. No matter how bad it looks, and this Chinese thing is as bad as they come, he will break into rope-a-dope.

"It never fails. Time passes. There's another scandal. Clinton's scandal or somebody else's, it doesn't matter. If it's somebody else's, they don't know the rules and they suck up and that takes the attention away from you. And guess what? The sky didn't fall, and the people say 'So what?' to glaring evidence that the president of the United State sold out to the Chinese."

There seems to be a new scandal, a new crisis, a new reason why the sky is falling each day in the Clinton administration. Despite all the revelations of wrongdoings, the public reacts with a "So what?" attitude, ignoring each of them. Larry says that reaction is by design, and that it comes from Clinton's skills as a pathological liar. He says that Clinton's ability to tell a lie with a straight face is his strength. "We used it to make him what he is," Larry said of his days on Clinton's damage control squad. "That's why he could be so good at all this stuff while he was so bad at everything else. No matter what Clinton got into, he could get out. The public reacts with a 'So what?' because we knew the game and how to play it to get that reaction.

"For example, we played rope-a-dope when things got hot. In no time at all, the press got off whatever was the hot problem and on to something else, and the people just forgot it that easy. All the presidents before Clinton didn't know the rules. Things got hot for them and they didn't understand rope-a-dope. Clinton knows that play, so remember when Filegate came along and everyone said the sky was falling? It was easy for Clinton to back off, get in a corner, hang in there, and let them take their punches. Sure enough, something else came along and the sky didn't fall. The people forgot Filegate real quick, so he's still there, we're still here, and the people say 'So what?' In the past, politicians would have something happen, people would say 'The sky is falling!' and the politicians would quit because they couldn't take the pain. Clinton has no pain. If he doesn't quit, and just takes it, even if the next item in the news that takes the public's mind off the Clinton scandal is another of his scandals, it doesn't matter. It takes their minds off it. This has happened so much that now the people just say 'So what?' with each new scandal."

Larry blames the Republican leadership for contributing to the "So what?" attitude throughout the country. He says Newt Gingrich and Trent Lott have sold their souls. The only way the Republican leaders can be brought back will be if the people demand it. He says, "We have politicians that are becoming like Bill Clinton instead of stopping him. The people expected them to put a stop to this, and instead they joined him."

It's Up to Kenneth Starr and You

There was a time when the Starr investigation was being attacked daily by the Clinton administration. The Democrats attacked and the Republicans claimed he was not moving fast enough. Virtually overnight, all the criticisms stopped simultaneously. With that change came the announcement by Starr that he had determined that Vince Foster died of a self-inflicted gunshot wound in Ft. Marcy Park.

I spoke out on the air and suggested that it appeared that Starr had sold out. His critics had become silent and he gave in to the prevailing damage control story about Foster. It looked like a deal was cut. I knew from Larry what evidence Starr had, so I knew that he knew Foster did not die in Ft. Marcy Park. It appeared that he lied.

Larry has always been a defender of Kenneth Starr's investigation. When we discussed this development he pointed out something very important, helping me to see that we may sometimes be too quick to judge. Starr had ended his Foster investigation because it was at a dead end and going nowhere. Evidence showed that he was killed somewhere else, but if

Starr were to make that claim he would also need to say where it happened and how. Those answers were not easily available. He moved the investigative staff from the Foster investigation to full-time pursuit of evidence surrounding Webster Hubbell. Larry had figured out that investigating Foster was getting Starr nowhere, but investigating Hubbell was the key to everything.

Unfortunately, there are detractors who only believe Larry when it is convenient for them to do so. Time and time again Larry has proven that his knowledge and insight are correct. Everything he has given has been fully substantiated. How often does he have to be right to violate all laws of chance?

One of his fans sent Larry a t-shirt with a cartoon style picture of him parting the Red Sea with Bill Clinton in a chariot charging toward him, about to be consumed by the returning waters. The t-shirt made me think of the reaction of people to his message in comparison to the reaction Moses got from his message. No matter how many miracles Moses performed, the people went back to their old ways and had to be continually reminded of what he taught them previously. No matter how often Larry has been right, people tend to disbelieve him each time something new comes out. They seem to keep forgetting his perfect track record.

His criticisms usually come from two sources. The first is obviously the people loyal to Bill Clinton who feel threatened and defensive. The other is from people who don't have his personal insight in to the Starr investigation and believe that Starr should be moving faster than he is. When Larry defends Starr, those people often attack Larry.

Larry tries to help everyone understand the technicalities of the investigative process. Prior to any indictments, Starr can question anyone with very little difficulty. Once an indictment takes place, then witnesses must be submitted to the court for approval, and the defendant's attorney can object and slow the process down for months. Because of this, Starr must make sure he has all the investigation and testimonies before handing out any indictments. Also, prior to the indictments, Starr has more flexibility to conduct discovery of evidence which may be only vaguely part of his jurisdiction. This enables him to collect evidence under oath which may assist in other investigations which may need to take place.

"So you can see what happens when they indict," says Larry. "They had better have their case made, because the minute they indict Hillary, all of this freewheeling is over. At that time they better have interviewed everyone they want to interview, because it is over the minute they indict. Right now the Clintons don't know who Starr's talking to. They don't know who I'm talking to. All of this is out there and the Clintons are very uncomfortable. They won't say that publicly of course, but they are very uncomfortable. They know we have some secret witnesses, but they don't know who they are, which means they don't know what Starr knows."

According to Larry, an impeachment hinges on the Republican leadership. Larry believes that an alliance has been formed between Republican leadership and Bill Clinton through the efforts of Dick Morris. He says that if Hillary is impeached (he believes she will be) and if evidence shows the president's involvement in illegal activities, the reaction of the Republican leadership will be a clue to whether he'll be impeached. Larry explained, "If they take the attitude that they want to leave it to the legal system to decide, then Clinton will come out of it.

"If they take the attitude of going straight forward into the impeachment part of it, then I think we will have the dynamics there to force Clinton out of office. I mean, I'm saying there's a good chance, not an absolute guarantee." Larry also believes that Clinton will rapidly lose support from his own party if evidence starts coming out so fast and in such quantity that Clinton's approval rating drops to an all-time low. If that happens, Larry predicts the Democrats will retreat from Clinton to avoid another major loss such as the one in 1994.

"And that's all we can do is try to force that day," explained Larry. "In my opinion, Bill Clinton is sick. He is mentally sick. He does not have the capability to know when it's over. When that day comes, he won't have the ability to figure it out. Hillary will know but he won't."

Larry will not quit. He has come a long way and believes that he is obligated to see his quest through or die trying. "I will expose Clinton," he says emphatically, "for the crimes he and Hillary have committed. I will do it. I have the evidence. I have the witnesses. I will do it with Kenneth Starr or without him.

"I can promise you this: if Starr stabs us in the back tomorrow, I'll keep going. I'll get somebody else. If the Republicans won't do it, I'll get somebody else. I'll just keep on. Why? Because time has no meaning. Maybe I don't have all the answers, but I'm farther along than anyone's ever gotten before. I may not have all the answers, but I've at least got most of them.

"I'm not saying being victorious in court, because that's out of my hands. It will be somebody else doing that. But just bringing them to justice considering everything that I've been up against is a coup all of its own. If people are smart, they will look at it and take heart and see that they could do the same thing at their local and state level. And hopefully enough people will start cleaning up corruption at all levels so that we don't ever have another Clinton."

9

Marching Orders

If you believe, as I do, that the warnings Larry Nichols has given us about the level of corruption in this country are to be taken seriously, then you have two courses of action you can pursue. The easiest is to do nothing and watch what is left of our country go down the drain. Or you can decide to take some action. Hopefully, you are willing to put forth some effort.

When I discussed this with Larry, he pointed out that "we're in a war. We're in a struggle for the soul of this nation. It's not a war in which we pick up guns and go to battle over some piece of ground. This is a war where the fight is one in which information is the weapon of choice." Of course, the weapons he offers in this information battle are his Nicholisms, to be used against the Clinton damage control squad.

Larry warns that "a juggernaut is rapidly coming across this land and is destroying the heart and fiber, even the very soul of this great nation. But because it is not an enemy everyone can see, most people don't know it is coming. Only after it hits will the effects be seen, and then it may be too late. We can stop it when we understand that the real threat is the damage control deception coming out of Washington, D.C. Once you know and understand the tactics being used to destroy us, you can help educate your neighbor. One by one we can build an army of Americans who know how to defend themselves. The only way to make that happen is to remember the Nicholism 'Everything starts with one.'"

First, it begins with you as the first "one." Then you must take action and share this book with others, or better yet, give extra copies to as many people as you can. Have them do the same. Before long we will have inoculated millions of Americans against the effects of damage control deception, the worst epidemic to ever hit our country.

Larry said, "I've got a lot of friends who are working awfully hard for this cause. It would be a mission impossible on its own, just fighting the people we have to fight. But it gets more difficult when you see what sometimes happens in a struggle like this. Clinton has all the money he needs to wage this battle because he tapped into the Communist Chinese and other questionable characters for millions."

Clinton's millions are tough to beat, but it can be done. When I was outspent three to one by my legislative opponent, I turned to the people. I went out and knocked on every door in my district and asked each person I met to help me. Grassroots politics, not money, enabled me to win. We can do the same thing on a larger scale to win our country back. Let this book be your new manual for battling the Clinton damage control squad. Take it door to door to friends, neighbors, and relatives. Get them to do the same. More can be done through grass roots action than with all the money in a Chinese bank.

Read this as often as needed to give you a firm understanding of the damage control methods it describes, as well as the Nicholisms to help you win the battle. Have discussions with others about what you've learned and help them to learn it too. Make it your priority every day to give out copies of the book, and have discussions about damage control and Nicholisms. With that kind of commitment, together we can teach the people of America about the danger they face. Together, we can teach them how to defend themselves.

"I travel all over this country and speak to many groups," Larry explained. "I always ask, 'How many of you are willing to lay your life down to save this county?' It's amazing the number of hands that go up in the air. But what is equally amazing is that those same people go home and the majority don't do anything about what I've taught them." Until now, no one really knew what to do next. The strategies in this book now give conservative Americans a way to bring about real change. If you put this book down and do nothing, Clinton, and those who are like him, win.

Appendix

Much of the evidence will never be known because many people who were witnesses or who possessed evidence of some kind suffered mysterious deaths prior to being able to come forward. The list compiled here is not complete and is not detailed. It is presented to show how extensive it is and to illustrate that all these deaths could not be just coincidence.

Following the list of names you will find a sample of some of the evidence Larry obtained by Larry. It is only intended to give you an idea of the type of documents he has obtained. This is merely a sample from his collection of a full forty boxes.

Mary Mahoney—former White House intern gunned down in a coffee shop. Nothing was taken. It was suspected that she was about to testify about sexual harassment in the White House.

Vincent Foster—former White House Counsel, found dead of a gunshot wound to the head and ruled a suicide. He had significant knowledge of the Clintons' financial affairs and was a business partner with Hillary. If the Clintons are guilty of the crimes they are accused of by Larry, Vincent Foster would have detailed knowledge of those crimes.

C. Victor Raiser, II—former National Finance Co-Chairman of Clinton for President, and *Montgomery Raiser*, his son. Both died in a suspicious private plane crash in Alaska. No cause determined. Raiser was considered to be a major player on the Clinton team.

Paul Tully—DNC Political Director, was found dead in a Little Rock hotel room. No cause was ever determined and no autopsy was allowed. Tully was a key member of the damage control squad and came up with some of the Clinton strategies.

Ed Willey—Clinton fund raiser. Found in the woods in Virginia with a gunshot wound to the head. Ruled a suicide.

Hershell Friday—Clinton fund-raiser. His plane exploded.

Jerry Parks—former security team member for Governor Clinton. Prior to his death he had compiled an extensive file on Clinton's activities. His family had reported being followed and his home was broken into just before being gunned down at a deserted intersection.

James Bunch—reported to have possessed a little black book of people who visited prostitutes. He died of a gunshot, which was ruled a suicide.

John Wilson—former Washington, D.C. council member. Had ties to Whitewater. Died of a very suspicious hanging suicide.

Kathy Ferguson—former wife of Arkansas State Trooper Danny Ferguson, the co-defendant with Bill Clinton in the Paula Jones lawsuit. Found dead in her living room of a gunshot wound to the head. Ruled a suicide. Interestingly, her packed suitcases seemed to indicate she was about to go somewhere.

Bill Shelton—Arkansas state trooper and fiancé of Kathy Ferguson. Allegedly committed suicide by shooting himself at her grave.

Gandy Baugh—attorney for Dan Lasater in a financial misconduct case. Supposedly jumped out the window of a tall building to commit suicide.

Dr. Donald Rogers—dentist. Killed in a suspicious plane crash on his way to an interview with reporter Ambrose Evans-Pritchard to reveal information about Clinton.

Stanley Huggins—lawyer investigating Madison Guaranty. Suicide. His extensive report has never been released.

Florence Martin—Accountant for the CIA and had information on the Barry Seal case. Three gunshot wounds to the head.

Suzane Coleman—reportedly had an affair with Clinton. Was seven months pregnant at the time she was found dead of a gunshot wound to the back of the head, ruled suicide.

Paula Grober—Clinton's interpreter for the deaf. Traveled with Clinton from 1978 until her death in 1992 in a one-car accident. There were no witnesses.

Paul Wilcher—attorney investigating corruption. He had investigated federal elections, drug and gun smuggling through Mena, the Waco incident, and had just delivered a lengthy report to Janet Reno. He died in his home of unknown causes.

Jon Parnell Walker—RTC investigator who mysteriously fell to his death from an apartment balcony.

Ron Brown—former DNC Chairman, Commerce Secretary. Reported to have died in a plane crash, but new evidence reveals he may have been shot in the head. He was being investigated by a special investigator and was about to be indicted with 54 others. He spoke publicly of his willingness to "make a deal" with the prosecutors. He is reported to have told Clinton that he would make a deal with the prosecutors to save himself a few days before the fatal trip. He was not supposed to be on the flight but was asked to go at the last minute.

Barbara Wise—Commerce Department secretary. Worked with Ron Brown and John Huang and had extensive knowledge of their activities. Found dead in her locked office the day after Thanksgiving. It was ruled a suicide. Interestingly, she was found partially clothed, bruised, and in a pool of blood.

Charles Meissner—Assistant Secretary of Commerce. John Huang was given a special security clearance by Meissner. Shortly thereafter, he died in the crash of a small plane.

Kevin Ives and *Don Henry*—seventeen-year-old boys who apparently saw something related to drugs in Mena by accident late at night. Officially ruled an accidental death on the train tracks, but evidence shows they died before being placed on the tracks—one of a crushed skull and the other of a knife wound in the back.

Keith Koney—had information on the Ives and Henry deaths. Died in a motorcycle accident with reports of a high-speed car chase involved.

Keith McKaskle—had information on the Ives and Henry deaths. Stabbed to death.

Gregory Collins—had information on the Ives and Henry deaths. Gunshot wound to the head.

Jeff Rhodes—had information on the Ives and Henry and

McKaskle deaths. Tortured, mutilated, shot, body burned in a dumpster.

James Milam—had information on the Ives and Henry deaths. He was decapitated. The coroner ruled death due to natural causes.

Jordan Kettleson—had information on the Ives and Henry deaths. Found shot in the front seat of his pick up truck.

Dr. Stanley Heard—Chair, National Chiropractic Health Care Advisory Committee. He personally treated Clinton's mother, stepfather, and brother. His personal small plane developed problems so he rented another. Fire broke out in flight and he crashed.

Steve Dickson—attorney for Heard. Died in same plane crash.

John Hillier—video journalist and investigator. He helped to produce the documentaries "Circle of Power," and "The Clinton Chronicles." He mysteriously died in a dentist's chair for no apparent reason.

Maj. Gen. William Robertson, Col. William Densberger, Col. Robert Kelly, Spec. Gary Rhodes, Steve Willis, Robert Williams, Conway LeBleu, Todd McKeehan, Sgt. Brian Haney, Sgt. Tim Sabel, Maj. William Barkley, Capt. Scott Reynolds—all former Clinton bodyguards who are dead.

Gary Johnson—former attorney for Larry Nichols, severely beaten and left for dead.

Dennis Patrick—had millions of dollars laundered through his account at Lasater & Co. without his knowledge. There have been several attempts on his life, all unsuccessful.

L.J. Davis—reporter. While investigating the Clinton scandals he was attacked in his hotel room and his notes were taken. He survived.

Larry Nichols—former marketing director of ADFA. Responsible for bringing forth more evidence and witnesses on Clinton corruption than any other source. Very public about his claims against Clinton. He has suffered six beatings, arrest on trumped up charges, and a near arrest.

Note: Larry Nichols, Larry Patterson, and David Bresnahan are all in fine health, they are not depressed, and they are not suicidal.

The following pages contain samples of the evidence Larry Nichols has obtained. The small format of this book makes them a bit difficult to read. To obtain a more legible sample of over fifty documents in 8.5 x 11 format, please send your request, along with $12.95, to:

Talk USA
Box 1168
West Jordan, UT 84084-7168.

2551

UNITED STATES GOVERNMENT
M E M O R A N D U M
U.S. SECRET SERVICE

DATE: 07/20/93   12:01 pm

REPLY TO

ATTN OF: SA SCOTT MARBLE

SUBJECT: DEATH OF VINCENT FOSTER, DEPUTY ASSISTANT TO THE PRESIDENT AND
          DEPUTY COUNSEL (SEE ATTACHED)

TO: SAIC INTELLIGENCE DIVISION

ON 7/20/93, AT 2130 HRS, LT WOLTZ, USSS/UD - WHD, CONTACTED THE ID/DD AND
ADVISED THAT AT 2030 HRS, THIS DATE, HE WAS CONTACTED BY LT GAVIN, US PARK
POLICE, WHO PROVIDED THE FOLLOWING INFORMATION:

ON THE EVENING OF 7/20/93, UNKNOWN TIME, US PARK POLICE DISCOVERED THE BODY
OF VINCENT FOSTER IN HIS CAR. THE CAR WAS PARKED IN THE FT. MARCY AREA OF VA
NEAR THE GW PARKWAY. MR. FOSTER APPARENTLY DIED OF A SELF-INFLICTED GUNSHOT
WOUND TO THE HEAD. A .38 CAL. REVOLVER WAS FOUND IN THE CAR.

SA TOM CANAVIT, WFO PI SQUAD, ADVISED THAT HE HAS BEEN IN CONTACT WITH US
PARK POLICE AND WAS ASSURED THAT IF ANY MATERIALS OF A SENSITIVE NATURE
(SCHEDULES OF THE POTUS, ETC.) WERE RECOVERED, THEY WOULD IMMEDIATELY BE
TURNED OVER TO THE USSS. (AT THE TIME OF THIS WRITING, NO SUCH MATERIALS WERE
LOCATED)

NO FURTHER INFORMATION AVAILABLE.

INVESTIGATION BY US PARK POLICE CONTINUING.

THE FOLLOWING NOTIFICATIONS WERE MADE BY USSS/UD - WHD:

DAVE WATKINS   DIR. OF PERSONNEL, WH
INSP. DENNIS MARTIN   USSS/UD
CRAIG LIVINGSTONE   WH SECURITY COORDINATOR
ASAIC PAUL IMBORDINO   CPO
DAD RICHARD GRIFFIN   CPO (BY ASAIC IMBORDINO)
ATSAIC DON FLYNN   PPD (BY ASAIC IMBORDINO)
SAIC RICHARD MILLER   PPD (BY ATSAIC FLYNN)
DIRECTOR MAGAW   DIR (BY DAD GRIFFIN)

THE FOLLOWING NOTIFICATIONS WERE MADE BY THE ID/DD:

ATSAIC LON WARFIELD   ID   2145 HRS
SAIC STEPHEN BERGER   ID   2150 HRS
DAD DALE WILSON   PA   2205 HRS
ASAIC CARL MEYER   PA   2217 HRS

                                                    6200

PLAINTIFF'S
EXHIBIT
3

AFFIDAVIT

State of Arkansas)
)
County of Pulaski   )

On this day comes before me, a Notary Public, authorized to administer oaths, in and for the County of Pulaski, State of Arkansas, Roger Perry to me well known, who being first duly sworn, says, upon oath:

On the 20th day of July, 1993, I received a telephone call from a person known to me as Helen Dickey. I was working on the security detail at the Arkansas Governor's mansion at Little Rock, Arkansas at that time. Dickey advised me that Vincent Foster, well knew to me had gotten off work and had gone out to his car in the parking lot and had shot himself in   the head. I do not recall the exact time of this telephone call but am fairly certain it was some time from about 4:30 p.m. to no later than 7:00 p.m.

Dickey had previously been employed as a baby-sitter for Governor Clinton's child and at the time of the call she was working at the White House in Washington, D.C. I then passed this message on to Governor Jim Guy Tucker through his wife.

During my tenure at the Governor's Mansion I received a number of calls from Jennifer Flowers to Governor Clinton.

I have been told by Danny Ferguson, another trooper who was working security detail at the time, at the Governor's Mansion, that he had talked with a young lady named Paula during a conference at the Excelsior Hotel and that he had taken her up to a room in that Hotel at the direct request of then Governor Bill Clinton. Danny has also stated that he talked with Paula at a restaurant in Little Rock during a chance meeting shortly before she filed her suit. He told her then, according to his conversation with me that he would testify in her behalf if she did file suit against Clinton. I have read Danny's answer to her suit and see that he admitted taking Paula up to Clinton's room on that occasion.

Roger L. Perry
Roger Perry, Affiant

Subscribed and sworn to before me this the 2x̲ᵗ̲ʰ̲ day of March, 1995.

Judith K. Washburn
Notary Public

My Commission Expires September 24, 2003

PLAINTIFF'S
EXHIBIT
4 A

AFFIDAVIT

State of Arkansas)
County of Pulaski)

On this day comes before me, a Notary Public, authorized to administer oaths, in and for the County of Pulaski, State of Arkansas, Larry Patterson, to me well known, who being first duly sworn, says, upon oath:

I received a telephone call from Roger Perry on the 20th day of July, 1993. Roger was working security detail at the Arkansas Governor's mansion at Little Rock. He advised me that a lady known to both of us as Helen Dickey had telephonically contacted him and advised him that Vincent Foster, well known to both of us because of his relationship with Hillary Clinton and his being an adviser to Governor Bill Clinton had gotten off work and had gone out to his car in the parking lot and had shot himself in the head. I do not recall the exact time of this telephone call but am fairly certain it was some time before 6:00 p.m on that date.

Dickey was employed as a baby-sitter by Governor and Hillary Clinton while in Arkansas and at the time of the call she was working at the White House in Washington, D.C.

I have been asked, under oath, whether Bill Clinton ever had extramarital affairs while he was Governor of Arkansas. I have replied that I knew Jennifer Flowers, who has said she had an affair with Governor Clinton. I took him, on occasions to the Quapaw Towers, where she lived, and where he would meet with her. I have taken him to see other females with whom he had personal relationships, including one he met during the night at Chelsea Clinton's schoolyard. I worked with Danny Ferguson, another trooper who was working security detail at the Governor's Mansion. Danny told me that he had talked with a young lady named Paula Jones during a meeting at the Excelsior Hotel in Little Rock. He told me he had taken her up to a room in that Hotel after having been asked to by then Governor Bill Clinton. On one occasion I was with Governor Clinton when we met Paula Jones in the rotunda at the State Capitol. The Governor referred to her as Paula as they hugged. Danny has also told me that he talked with Paula at a restaurant in Little Rock in the summer of 1994. At that time, Paula told Danny that she had learned she had been mentioned in a magazine article about Bill Clinton. He told her then, according to his conversation with me, that he would testify in her behalf if she did file suit against Clinton. I have read Danny's answer to her suit and see that he admitted taking Paula up to Clinton's room on that occasion. That agrees with what I know about that situation.

Larry Patterson, Affiant

Subscribed and sworn to before me this the _24th_ day of March, 1995.

Judith K. Washburn
Notary Public

My Commission Expires: _September 24, 2003_

PLAINTIFF'S
EXHIBIT
4B

This is to certify that on the 20th day of July, 1993, I received a telephone call from Roger Perry, of the Arkansas State Police, who was a member of the Arkansas Governor's Security Staff.

Perry advised me that he had just received a telephone call from one Helen Dickey, a former baby-sitter for Chelsea Clinton, who was employed at the White House and that she had advised him that Vincent Foster, known to both Perry and me, had gone to his car on the parking lot and had shot himself in the head.

I do not recall the exact time of the call but I place it as being during the rush hour at the White House and assumed there must be many witnesses to the event. Perry advised me that Dickey was quite upset as if the event had happened shortly before her call to him. I estimate the time as being no later than six o'clock, Central Standard Time.

Perry advised me that he had telephonically contacted Betty Tucker who had relayed the message to Governor Jim Guy Tucker.

Lynn A. Davis
Lynn A. Davis

3..24-95
Date

Sworn & subscribed to:
Kathy L. Thornton Notary
Pulaski Co. exp 5-9-99

CRIMINAL INVESTIGATION SECTION

INTELLIGENCE

CIS - 3C
DATE: 3/22/76
DICTATED BY: INV. DOUG FOGLEY
COUNTY: Washington
SOURCE OF INFORMATION: ███████████████
TOPIC OF INFORMATION: Criminal Activity
DATE TYPED: 3/25/76
COPIES TO: CAPT. GEORGE MOYE
                               LT. CARROLL EVANS
                               INV. FOGLEY

<u>VERY CONFIDENTIAL</u>

This information was related to this agent on the morning of March 22, 1976 by Sheriff HERB MARSHALL.

No dissemination is to be made of this information other than to this agent, Captain MOYE and Lieutenant EVANS.

Several hotels in the southern United States including Arkansas are owned by the Teamsters Union as legitimate businesses which the various factions of the somewhat questionable Teamsters Union use to "clean" their money. Two such hotels are the Downtowner Inn in Fayetteville and the Aristocrat Hotel in Hot Springs. The Teamsters Union goes out of its way to keep these hotels highly legitimate and of unquestionable reputation. The manager or overseerer employed by the Teamsters Union for the two hotels in Arkansas (plus others) is BOB FORSHEE, a white male. Recently a private club called the Brass Monkey was established in the basement of the Downtowner Inn in Fayetteville, Arkansas. This club of somewhat questionable reputation has lately caused the Teamsters certain anxiety about it being in one of their hotels. The club is leased and the license holder for the private club are DON TYSON, a white male and BILLIE SNYDER, a white female.

DON TYSON needs no introduction to the State Police CID or for that matter any law enforcement agency in Northwest, Arkansas. He is an extremely wealthy man with much political influence and seems to be involved in most every kind of shady operation especially narcotics, however, has to date gone without implication in any specific crime. TYSON likes

FILE NUMBER: N L I-2465

CRIMINAL INVESTIGATION DIVISION

INTELLIGENCE

CID- 3C
DATE: October 24, 1980
DICTATED BY: INVESTIGATOR TAYLOR
COUNTY: WASHINGTON
SOURCE OF INFORMATION: CONFIDENTIAL INFORMANT
TOPIC OF INFORMATION: NARCOTICS TRAFFIC/HOMICIDE
DATE TYPED: October 29, 1980
COPIES TO: INVESTIGATOR TAYLOR
                               LIEUTENANT EVANS
                               SERGEANT STEPHENS

     The following information was received from a confidential
source whose reliabilty has not been established at this time.

     Dissemination of this information is restricted.

     The confidential source related to me that they had been
present at a party in Washington County when a drug deal was
being made. They advised Sheriff HERB MARSHALL, DON TYSON, HAROLD
JONES, RONNIE TEAGUE, and a subject by the name of MONTEZ who
was also present.

     They also related that they had been told on Monday, after
GAIL VAUGHT was killed that she was unconscious when she was
killed. They also related that they had been told that a RAY
FOREMAN had confessed to Sheriff MARSHALL that he had run over
GAIL, but it was an accident, for they were both high on Acid.
They also related that they had been told that RAY FOREMAN had
failed three polygraph tests.

NO DISSEMINATION

TO: Taylor   DATE ____
TO: Evans   DATE ____
TO: Stephens   DATE ____
TO: Fogley   DATE ____
TO: CIFOTO   DATE ____
TO: _____   DATE ____
TO: _____   DATE ____
TO: _____   DATE ____
TO: _____   DATE ____
TO: _____   DATE ____

I-H835
I-7465

FILE NUMBER:

B-2

TYPED
INDEXED
LOGGED
PROOFED
QUAL. CON.
COPIED
FILED

CRIMINAL INVESTIGATION SECTION

INTELLIGENCE

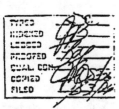

CIS - 3C	
DATE:	3/22/76
DICTATED BY:	INV. DOUG FOGLEY
COUNTY:	Washington
SOURCE OF INFORMATION:	[redacted]
TOPIC OF INFORMATION:	Criminal Activity
DATE TYPED:	3/25/76
COPIES TO:	CAPT. GEORGE MOYE LT. CARROLL EVANS INV. FOGLEY

VERY CONFIDENTIAL

This information was related to this agent on the morning of March 22, 1976 by Sheriff HERB MARSHALL.

No dissemination is to be made of this information other than to this agent, Captain MOYE and Lieutenant EVANS.

Several hotels in the southern United States including Arkansas are owned by the Teamsters Union as legitimate businesses which the various factions of the somewhat questionable Teamsters Union use to "clean" their money. Two such hotels are the Downtowner Inn in Fayetteville and the Aristocrat Hotel in Hot Springs. The Teamsters Union goes out of its way to keep these hotels highly legitimate and of unquestionable reputation. The manager or overseerer employed by the Teamsters Union for the two hotels in Arkansas (plus others) is BOB FORSHEE, a white male. Recently a private club called the Brass Monkey was established in the basement of the Downtowner Inn in Fayetteville, Arkansas. This club of somewhat questionable reputation has lately caused the Teamsters certain anxiety about it being in one of their hotels. The club is leased and the license holder for the private club are DON TYSON, a white male and BILLIE SNYDER, a white female.

DON TYSON needs no introduction to the State Police CID or for that matter any law enforcement agency in Northwest, Arkansas. He is an extremely wealthy man with much political influence and seems to be involved in most every kind of shady operation especially narcotics, however, has to date gone without implication in any specific crime. TYSON likes

FILE NUMBER: I-2465

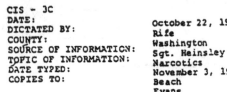

CRIMINAL INVESTIGATION SECTI

INTELLIGENCE

CIS - 3C
DATE: October 22, 1976
DICTATED BY: Rife
COUNTY: Washington
SOURCE OF INFORMATION: Sgt. Heinsley
TOPIC OF INFORMATION: Narcotics
DATE TYPED: November 3, 1976
COPIES TO: Beach
                                 Evans
                                 Rife

On 10/21/76, Sergeant HERBERT HEINSLEY,
who has furnished information before and · reliability
is apparent gave this investigator the following Information.
A ▇▇▇▇▇▇▇▇▇▇, who is a white female and is employed
at the County Collector's office in Mountain Home,
Arkansas under a federal grant advised that approximately
2 months ago, she and another white female ROBBIE
CORNELIUS who is a girlfriend of DON TYSON, and has
a child by MR. TYSON went to Fayetteville, Arkansas
to see DON TYSON and they stayed at a motel for 3
days. She stated that the reason she didn't get
back in just one day was that she had to bring the
car back. She advised that when they first went to Springdale
they went to TYSON'S office and TYSON gave ROBBIE
a wad of bills and when they got out to where they could
count them it amounted to $600. After getting a room
at the motel in Springdale, ROBBIE left and stayed all
night with some old man who owns horses and lives at
Fayetteville. Then the next night, ROBBIE supposedly
spent the night with DON TYSON.

▇▇▇▇▇▇▇ indicated that from other things
that she learned while on that trip with ROBBIE CORNELIUS
She is afraid that she might get killed as she understands
that DON TYSON is a drug dealer and brings the drugs in
from California by truck and also airplanes.

She advised that DON TYSON moved ROBBIE CORNELIUS
to Little Rock and that after she got busted and ▇▇▇▇▇▇
thinks that DON TYSON set ROBBIE up to get rid of her in
this matter. She admits and DON TYSON also admitted that
the child of ROBBIE CORNEILIUS belongs to DON TYSON.

▇▇▇▇▇▇▇▇▇ is associated with the drug
crowd in Mountain Home, Arkansas and works part time
as a bar maid at a local eating place called The Farm.

FILE NUMBER: I· 7465

CRIMINAL INVESTIGATION DIVISION

INTELLIGENCE

CID - 3C
DATE: 2-5-80
DICTATED BY: INV. DON SANDERS
COUNTY: WASHINGTON --
SOURCE OF INFORMATION: CONFIDENTIAL INFORMANT
TOPIC OF INFORMATION: DRUG TRAFFICKING
DATE TYPED: 2-8-80
COPIES TO: INV. SANDERS

NO DISSEMINAT...

On 2-6-80, Investigator Sanders along with
SA Bob Morris interviewed a confidential source
at the FBI office in Fayetteville, AR, relative
to Drug trafficking in the DON TYSON FOOD COMPANY.

The reliability of this information is
unknown and dissemination should be restricted
to CID personnel.

The CI advised that several individuals
whom he refused to identify, are distributing
amphetamines to the personnel in TYSON FOOD
COMPANY, mostly truck drivers. The source
further stated the pills were being brought in
on TYSON's business plane. However the source
did state that he had only been told this,
although he had personally used the drugs himself.
The informant alleged that deliveries were being
made on a weekly basis and that the pills
are contained in quart jars sealed with paraffin.

The source did not know whether or not
DON TYSON is responsible for the pills or if they
were being brought in by TYSON personnel. The
CI did agree to provide samples of the pills
at a future date for analysis due to recent
counterfeiting of controlled substances in pill
forms. The source declined to provide any
additional information until a future date.

TO: _____ DATE
TO: CIF 010 DATE
TO: _____ DATE
TO: _____ DATE
TO: _____ DATE
TO: _____ DATE
TO: _____ DATE
TO: _____ DATE
TO: _____ DATE
TO: _____ DATE

FILE NUMBER: 1-7885

B-23

About the Author

Early in his career, David Bresnahan, 44, was a radio station news director, then a reporter and photographer at daily papers in the New England area. Recently he hosted a daily talk radio show on KTKK radio in Salt Lake City, where he was the general manager and sales manager. Bresnahan presently hosts the nationally syndicated show "Talk USA Investigative Reports" and has published his own internet web site at *http://talkusa.com*.

Interestingly, Bresnahan spent more than twenty years of his life involved in the sport of gymnastics. He not only took part in NCAA competition himself, but he was also an accomplished coach and international judge. In 1986 he was selected to coach the U.S. Men's Gymnastics Team for two competitions in the Soviet Union. He speaks frequently to church, youth, and business groups, offering motivational and inspirational messages.

Bresnahan received a B.S. in Communications from Westminster College of Salt Lake City, along with a minor in computer science.

In 1994, Bresnahan was elected to serve in the Utah House of

Representatives as a Republican, where he distinguished himself by sponsoring legislation to ban both partial birth and saline solution abortions. That bill passed and is in effect in Utah, the first state in the nation to do so successfully. He served on the Transportation and Public Safety Appropriations Committee, the Business, Labor and Economic Development Standing Committee, as well as the Human Services Standing Committee.